# Over the River and Through the Woods ...

## Recipes from Grandma's House

By Pat Harris and Nevonne McDaniels

Thanks to my co-author Nevonne McDaniels. I couldn't have done it without you. Also, to grandson Adam Granzer, for your help with the photo equipment. And, of course, to the tasters – husband Neval, Kelly, Adam and friends – and the rest of the family who have been so encouraging.

To my children, grandchildren and great-grandchildren, I hope you all enjoy the cookbook.

Written with love,
Pat Harris
(*aka Mom, Mutter, Grandma*)

Copyright © 2018 by Natapoc Mountain Press LLC
Plain, Washington
ISBN / 13 978-1718901186
Printed by CreateSpace, an Amazon.com Company

Painting of house on the cover by Kristen McCurdy

# Table of Contents

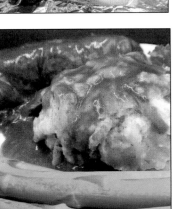

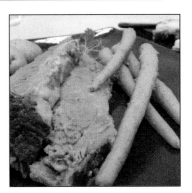

*Over the River ...*

# 'Make the most of what you have and be prepared to improvise'

### By Pat Harris

The introduction I wrote for the "The Red Cabin Cookbook" (1981) was about The Old Woman and the Shoe *(see next page)*. Now, 35-plus years later, I'm probably more like Old Mother Hubbard, whose cupboard is anything but bare.

After publishing the first cookbook, it took some time, but eventually I again started looking for ways to keep boredom at bay.

My husband retired from logging and turned his attention to farming, so his schedule was more flexible. The kids were grown and out of the house (though they — and some of the grandkids — returned for extended stays from time to time) and the red cabin, where I had operated the bakery, had burned down, limiting some self-employment options.

When I heard the YMCA Camp at Lake Wenatchee was looking for a summer camp cook, I thought that might do the trick.

It was similar to what I had been doing at home, just more of it. We served breakfast, lunch and dinner three or four days a week for 40 to 100 kids, ages 10 to 13, plus high school counselors and some adults.

Jeff Meredith, the manager at the time, was a great boss. He never told me what to do. He said, "This is your kitchen. Do what you want." He would stop by and sample. He did a lot of sampling.

The experience opened up opportunities for other endeavors during the next two decades or so.

I leased a restaurant space in Plain and ran "Pat's Place" for a couple of years. I worked in the kitchen at the hospital in Leavenworth, where I learned more about different types of diets and nutrition. I worked as the cook at a mountain-top resort, which intro-

My birthday ride with grandson Adam, on my 86th birthday. It was a fast trip on his Kawasaki Ninja ZX6R.

duced me to "country gourmet" cooking (and how to ride a snowmobile). Several recipes included in this cookbook were created for the resort guests and later incorporated into our family dinners. This collection also includes recipes and techniques I learned as a prep cook at a German restaurant in Leavenworth that featured authentic German cuisine under the direction of an actual German.

Each job challenged me in different ways and broadened my experience. When I got into my 70s, I quit working outside the home, but continued (and still continue) to provide meals and care for a household that has gone from five or six people to three or four people, depending on the day, with spurts of up to 15 or more for special occasions.

A couple of years ago I realized

just how many "new" recipes had worked their way into our family get-togethers.

"Is this in the cookbook?" the grandchildren would ask.

"Nope," I would answer. "It's in my head."

"You should write another," they would say.

So, I did, with some help. "Over the River and Through the Woods: Recipes from Grandma's House" is the result.

As for the moral of the story of Old Mother Hubbard, it's probably not far off from that of The Old Woman and Shoe, "If you live in a comfortable old shoe with a comfortable old man, give the old man the attention he needs and keep busy, and live happily ever after."

I would add, "Make the most of what you have and be prepared to improvise."

# The Old Woman and The Shoe

*(From The Red Cabin Cookbook)*

There was an old woman who lived in a shoe. She had many children, but she did know what to do. She loved them, sewed for them and cooked for them. After 35 years of this, the children all left to live in their own shoes. The old woman looked around and found the big shoe very empty. She wasn't really alone because the old man who lived in the old shoe was there. The years the old woman was busy with the children, the old man was out in the woods working so that the children and the old woman had the things they needed.

Now that the old man could have more attention from the old woman, the old man would still go to work, leaving the old woman alone in the big old shoe, feeling like she wasn't needed anymore. The hands that had been so busy for so long, sewing and cooking, were idle most of the time. The old woman was not happy with idle hands.

She listened to the folks who said that women should go to school or to work when their children leave the shoe. But the old man liked to have her at home, and the old woman liked to be there. The old man's routine hadn't changed, but the old woman felt a terrible emptiness in her life. The old woman finally decided that she was the only one who could solve her problem. The old man was very nice to the old woman, but he didn't know how to help her.

One day she said to the old man, "I really need to have something to do. I can sew, so maybe I can sew some things to sell, and it will give me some-thing to do, so that the old shoe won't seem so empty."

She fixed up the red cabin next to the old shoe and started a sewing shop. She made some clothes for some ladies and some bonnets that she sold in some stores. After a while, she thought she needed more to do so she made some homemade bread. Soon she was really busy selling bonnets and homemade bread.

Everyone liked what she made but after several years the old woman found out that it was a very hard job for an old woman, so she closed the bakery and was again without enough to keep her from feeling like she was of no use.

She thought and thought. Finally, she decided that since her children had asked for her recipes for their families in their own shoes, she would make them a

*By* Pat Harris

*This cookbook stays open! See page 4*

book with all of the recipes she had used through the years and give them each a copy.

The old woman sorted and copied recipes for the children she loved so much and was happy again. She worked for several years and finally felt that she had everyone's favorite recipes in the book. When the children and the old woman's friends that lived in the old shoe's neighborhood heard about the book, they all said, "such a fine collection of recipes should be shared."

So the old woman published the book and called it "The Red Cabin Cookbook."

The old man and the old woman still live in the old shoe, and the old woman is still finding things she can do. The children come to visit in the old shoe and the children from the neighbors' shoes come to visit, too.

The moral of the story is if you live in a comfort-able old shoe with a comfortable old man, give the old man the attention he needs and keep busy, and live happily ever after.

# Menus

*Food and family go hand-in-hand. It doesn't take long for a menu thrown together one year to become tradition. That doesn't mean you shouldn't mix it up once in a while. What follows are some of our family's favorite menus (and a few stories to go with them) as well as suggestions for things to try when you're looking to get out of the rut.*

## Little Grandma's Chicken Dinner Picnic

### Dinner

Grandma's
Chicken
*(Page 80)*

Potato Salad
*(Page 44)*

Pea Pods

Watermelon

### Dessert

Apple Kuchen
*(Page 109)*

**L**ittle Grandma was my dad's mother.

We called her "Little Grandma" because she was just barely 5 feet tall (as opposed to Big Grandma, my mother's mother, who must have been about 5-foot-6). We started the nicknames when we were kids. We never thought about last names, just Big Grandma and Little Grandma.

Little Grandma was a good cook.

She (Mary Clerf) originally came from Luxembourg. Her family owned a gasthaus there.

*(I visited there in 2005, with my granddaughter Kimberly and cousin Guy Clerf and his family. It's still a gasthaus, but the family doesn't own it anymore.)*

She immigrated to the United States in 1901, settling in Wisconsin, which is where she met Grandpa (William Vey). He had been a soldier in the Prussian army. He emigrated from Prussia in 1891.

After they married, they came to the Seattle area for work. Eventually he got a job working for the city of Seattle, though I'm not sure what he did.

She and my grandfather later moved to a ranch in Maple Valley. They had chickens, raised their own pigs and had a milk cow. They raised their own beef. They were very self-sufficient.

They cut hay with a scythe, the hard way, and brought it to the barn with a horse and wagon. They put the hay loose in the barn and would salt it. The grandkids' job was to pack it down. We would climb up in the rafters

# Backyard Spread

## Dinner

Potato Pie
(Page *103*)

Barbecue Ribs
(Page *71*)

Green Salad

## Dessert

Cream Cheese
Pie
(Page *118*)

Little Grandma (Mary Clerf Vey) and Wilhelm Vey on their wedding day in 1901. They later had a farm in Maple Valley.

and then jump on it. We thought that was a good job.

When Grandpa milked the cow, if we were quiet, we could stand in the doorway and watch. He would say, "Open your mouth," and we would all open our mouths and he would squirt the milk at us. He was a good shot, but sometimes we ended up with milk all over.

My dad would go up and help butcher the pigs in the fall.

They would grind some of the meat, fry it and then put it in crocks, with layers of lard between the meat. That's how they preserved it. The lard sealed it. They must have had an underground cellar or something. This was before everyone had a refrigerator and a freezer.

During the butchering, Little Grandma would fix huge breakfasts. Our family was there, and my uncle and all his family.

She would make plate-sized pancakes, a big stack of them, along with fried potatoes, milk gravy and sausage. A sturdy breakfast. She made her own syrup, boiling down sugar and water and flavoring.

Aunt Rose on the farm in Maple Valley.

During the summers, Aunt Rose (Little Grandma's youngest daughter – my dad's little sister) would pick us all up and take us to a resort on Lake Wilderness in Maple Valley, on picnics. Little Grandma would make a big batch of her chicken and potato salad. And we would have watermelon, cantaloupe and lemonade.

We would all go, maybe eight or 10 kids altogether with all the cousins.

*Over the River ...*

# Roast Chicken

## Dinner
Roast Chicken
with Rice
Stuffing
*(Page 86)*

Baked Beans

Spinach Salad

The resort had a big slide into the water – not like the waterslides now, where they have water running down them. We would climb up the ladder with a bucket of water and dump it on the slide before we slid down.

Grandpa and Little Grandma had four boys and a girl. My dad, Del, was next to the oldest. The boys must have been teenagers when Rose was born in 1920. They moved to the farm when Rose was 7, I think, so they were there when the Depression started.

Dad always said I started the Depression. I was born in 1929.

"Pat started it," he would say.

Our family lived on a houseboat until I was about 7.

The family at that time included my parents, Del and Lila, and four children, including my sister who died when she was 3.

She was born with an enlarged heart and was always sickly. It

Little Grandma, Big Grandma and my youngest brother Jerry.

was our job to make sure she had blankets under her so she wasn't cold. We were taught to take care of her. My dad was convinced that being on the water is what killed her, so we moved into a house two blocks up off the water. My youngest siblings, Jerry and Sandy, were born there.

Jobs were scarce, so Dad took whatever jobs he could find. He worked for the WPA during the Depression. He called it the Whistle Piss and Argue.

They dug ditches and built roads. It was good. It gave people the chance to work. They didn't make much, but it was better than doing nothing.

And Dad fished. We lived near the ship canal that runs from Lake Union to Ballard, through the government locks. Dad would row his boat through the locks and catch fish.

In those days it was mostly King

# What do you feed the kids when the cupboard is bare?

*(From the Red Cabin Cookbook)*

Cooking for a large family during the Depression years was quite a challenge. It took imagination and was a frustrating job trying to put meals on the table when you had no choice of ingredients. You used what food you could scrape up.

I grew up in the Depression and never remember being hungry. My mom always seemed to fill us up. The things I remember tasting so good don't taste that good to me now. An example: We were always hungry when we got home from school and went straight to the pantry to see what we could scare up. One of my favorite snacks was to take a slice of bread, pour canned milk on it and sprinkle it with sugar. Doesn't sound at all good to me now. My other favorite was to take a glass of milk and break up soda crackers in it. I still like that.

I think if there is one thing I remember eating the most, it was milk gravy. We had milk gravy on biscuits, potatoes, rice, bread and it is still a favorite. Salmon had to be second. My dad fished a lot and we ate salmon fried, baked, creamed … mom must have canned hundreds of quarts of salmon.

We went to grade school, not far from home, and walked home for lunch. Mom would have a big pot of hot cocoa made and a big stack of toast made out of homemade bread. I didn't know then that the toast was buttered with lard and sprinkled with salt. It tasted great. We always dunked it in our cocoa.

When I was a kid I wasn't too interested in messing around in the kitchen. My sister, Blanche, liked it. She could make a good cake when she was still in grade school. I wanted to try one time, but I ate so much of the dough while mixing it up that there wasn't enough left to bake. It was a lot of years later before I tried again.

I was a skinny kid. Dad always said that it was because I ate so much and got skinny carrying it around. He may have been right, too. We ate a lot of corn meal mush, rice with canned milk and sugar, hot cakes and biscuits and milk gravy.

We were raised in the city, but always had a large garden and chickens, so we had a pretty good diet, probably better than a lot of kids today, with the junk food so many eat. We had to work in the garden and carry in stove wood, so we got lots of exercise. We lived on, or near, the water, so we swam a lot. It seemed there were never enough hours in the day to do everything there was to do.

Salmon. Dad would catch fish and Mom would can them or he would trade them for other things.

Mom would fix the salmon a hundred ways. We ate a lot of salmon. We ate a lot of whatever you could get that didn't cost a lot of money.

We had a garden and chickens. Dad would go to the bakeries and get the bread they would throw out, telling them it was for the chickens.

He would bring home gunnysacks full and dump them out and we would pick out the good stuff for us to eat. The chickens would get what was left.

They would sell eggs, 10 cents a dozen.

We used to get free clothes, too. They had people who volunteered to make clothes. You would get a dress. Girls didn't wear long pants, but the dresses had underpants that matched. They always had a pocket in the underpants to put your hanky in.

We had garter belts. In the winter we wore these long brown stockings with garter belts to hold them up.

When the war came, Dad got a job building a dam somewhere near Snoqualmie Pass.

His oldest brother, Uncle Dewitt, who died of tuberculosis when he was fairly young, taught Dad how to do plumbing, so then he would get jobs as a pipe fitter and eventually became a full-fledged plumber.

After he started making money, he bought all kinds of things – a refrigerator and an electric stove. And there was no more skimping on food.

Salmon, split pea soup, all kinds of beans, pot roast, fried potatoes, corn bread, biscuits and chicken. Those are the kinds of things we grew up eating. I wasn't introduced to any other kind of food for a long time.

Dad enjoyed fishing even when the family wasn't depending on the food. My sons Bud and Bill caught the fishing bug, too.

## Tuesday Night Twist

### Dinner

Stuffed Meat Roll

*(Page 96)*

Pasta Salad

*(Page 42)*

Marinated Tomatoes

*(Page 101)*

### Dessert

Watermelon

This is an alternative to traditional meatloaf when you're looking for something a little different. You could serve it with the more traditional potatoes and hot vegetable. We combined it here with pasta salad and marinated tomatoes, which can be a fix-ahead summer meal.

We served these marinated tomatoes over a lettuce leaf as the tomato salad when I worked as the prep cook in the German restaurant in Leavenworth. It was paired with the schnitzel. Now this recipe is my go-to side dish, especially when we have garden fresh tomatoes in the summer.

The restaurant menu also included rouladen (page 89) and potato pancakes (page 24). The owner was German, so the recipes were his and I suppose as authentic as it's going to get.

# Impress the Guests

## Appetizer
Spinach Dip
with crackers and olives
*(Page 39)*

## Dinner
Shrimp and Halibut
Vol-au-vent
*(Page 93)*

Salad

## Dessert
Rum Cake
*(Page 131)*

**S**hrimp and Halibut Vol-au-vent is another of the "Country Gourmet" recipes from the lodge. We used a fish-shaped cutter made especially for vol-au-vents, with an inner blade that didn't cut clear through the puff pastry, making it easier to separate the inside layer. It was slick, but you don't need the cutter. This is a favorite of my granddaughters Jenny and Kimberly and daughter-in-law Trish.

I made the Spinach Dip recipe after one of the kids brought some to a family dinner. I thought I could do it better, so started playing, trying a few different things. Whenever I see something and I think I can make it better, I try it. That's what's fun about cooking.

As for the Rum Cake, a favorite of Nevonne's, it was in the Red Cabin Cookbook. I'm not sure where we got it originally, but it was about the time when Nevonne was in college and we were doing rum-soaked watermelons.

*Over the River ...*

## Favorite Birthday Dinner

*(Thanks to Hildegard)*

### Appetizer
Cheese and Grape Spears

### Dinner
Sour Bratwurst
*(Page 94)*

Cabbage – German Style
*(Page 99)*

German Potato Salad
*(Page 42)*

Melon

Green Salad

Homemade Bread
*(Page 50)*

### Dessert
Pumpkin Pudding
*(Page 129)*

The rule at our house is you get to pick the dinner and dessert menu for your birthday dinner. This bratwurst and onion mix, which came from my daughter-in-law Hildegard, along with pumpkin pie or pumpkin pudding, became my son Neval's favorite.

The birthday dessert requests seem to go through phases. We had a couple of years when chocolate pudding cake and banana cake were all the rage.

Then, Neval started requesting pumpkin pie for his birthday in July. We always had a big crowd for his parties, so I would make the "pie" in a sheet cake pan. It weighed 15 pounds.

I can't even remember how much pumpkin I used or how long it took to bake.

Of course, in his role as birthday boy, he cut the first piece — from the middle, a technique the grandkids adopted for later cake-cuttings.

A couple of years ago, when my two sons-in-law Kelly and Gary couldn't have flour, but still wanted pumpkin pie, I made pumpkin pudding, which is basically the same thing, without the crust. That soon became the new favorite.

We still have pumpkin pie for Thanksgiving and Christmas as well. Always. It's one of the family comfort foods.

My oldest son, John, lives in Germany and I have made several trips to visit him. The first time, in 1980, he wanted me to make pumpkin pie, one of those tastes of home unavailable there.

The Germans don't eat pumpkin. They feed it to the pigs. So, finding the ingredients was the first challenge. He ended up going to the PX to buy it. But I made the pie.

While I was there, I swapped some recipes with his wife's mother, Frau Steinbauer.

She spoke no English and I spoke no German, just part of the challenge. Instead of measuring cups, they measure dry ingredients by weight. So, I sat in her kitchen with a coffee cup, a teaspoon, a tablespoon and paper and pen. She would weigh out the flour for her recipe and then I would take it and measure it with the cup.

We did that with every ingredient. Some were easier than others. With the baking powder, for instance, she had pre-measured packets, which made it easier to figure out.

Once that was done, we had to convert temperatures. But that's how we translated those first recipes. It's easier now.

Hildegard, of course, speaks English, so she was able to give me the directions for the sour bratwurst during one of our weekly Skype conversations.

# Kelly's St. Patrick's Day Birthday Dinner

## Dinner
Corned Beef with Mustard Glaze
(Page **74**)

Brussels Sprouts

Cabbage, carrots and onions

Irish Soda Bread
(Page **61**)

## Dessert
Carrot Pineapple Cake
(Page **112**)

# Aunt Della's Italian Meatball Dinner

## Dinner
Meatballs, Sauce & Pasta
*(Page 82)*

Bread
*(Page 50)*

Green Salad with Blue Cheese Dressing
*(Page 43)*

Asparagus

## Dessert
Ice Cream Pie
*(Page 121)*

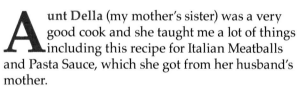

**A**unt Della (my mother's sister) was a very good cook and she taught me a lot of things including this recipe for Italian Meatballs and Pasta Sauce, which she got from her husband's mother.

His parents were Italian. They lived in Seattle, but had come from the old country and didn't speak much English. I think he was born here, though.

He was well-educated and worked as an accountant. Before the war, he worked for the railroad in Alaska and they ran a boarding house. Aunt Della cooked for all the guests, including railroad executives who passed through. They moved back to Seattle when the war started.

She was great. Everything she did, she did well. She would crochet dresses and suits. She could crochet anything.

She is the one who taught me how to make pie crust and how to budget, setting a percentage for housing and food. And she taught me how to cook good things cheap, like getting five meals from one large roast.

I was 16 when I got married. I had never been interested in learning to cook. I didn't even know how to make coffee.

I learned one thing at a time, usually the hard way. Sometimes I would ask for advice. But, not always.

The first bread I made, I had found a recipe, I'm not sure where, in a newspaper or someplace, and I thought, "I can make this. I'm going to learn to make bread."

So, I followed the recipe exactly, or so I thought. I mixed and kneaded it and raised it the first time. That worked out fine.

I punched it down, made two loaves and put them in bread pans. I was following the recipe closely. It did not say to raise it again once it was in the pans and I didn't know any better. It just said to bake it.

They turned out hard as a rock. I was so disgusted, I threw them out in the yard for our dog who had experience with cleaning up my cooking disasters. He would eat anything — except for that bread.

The boys, Tex and Bud, who were 3 and 4, or so at the time, had a sand pile out in the yard where they played with their little cars and trucks. They got hold of those loaves and used them for the rest of the summer to make roads in their sand pile.

I must have told someone what happened and they explained that you have to raise it again in the pan. After that I did a little better.

But most of what I learned, I learned by making a lot of mistakes. Information wasn't as easy to come by unless you were taught by someone, which I wasn't.

Besides, I always wanted to do it myself. I like the challenge, I guess. And I enjoy learning new things.

# Easter Dinner

## Appetizers

Stuffed
Mushrooms
*(Page 39)*

Deviled Eggs
*(Page 38)*

## Dinner

Roast
Leg of Lamb
*(Page 86)*

Minted Peas

Mashed Yams
*(Page 101)*

## Dessert

Lemon
Meringue Pie
*(Page 123)*

# Company's Coming

## Dinner

Paysanne Fillets
(halibut or salmon)
*(Page 84)*

Buttered Noodles
with Parmesan

Green Salad
Cottage Cheese and Fruit

## Dessert

Rhubarb Custard Pie
*(Page 130)*

# Cod with Peppers

## Dinner

Cod with Peppers
*(Page 73)*

Tater Tots

Green Salad

Blue Cheese Dressing
*(Page 43)*

## Dessert

Lemon Pie Cake
*(Page 122)*

I've never used a lot of processed, frozen foods, but we do have a few that appeared in later years. As the family got smaller, I started taking shortcuts. Tater Tots is one of those. They were a favorite.

And on shopping days, I would sometimes buy frozen chicken pot pies and fix them for a "lazy housewife" dinner.

## Soup for Dinner

### Dinner

Bean and Kale Soup

*(Page 46)*

Crusty Bread

*(Page 50)*

### Dessert

Nantucket Pudding

*(Page 126)*

Soup and homemade bread make a nice change for dinner. I make big pots of soup and freeze them in small containers. It makes for a quick lunch or dinner for those hectic days.

Incorporating beans in your diet is good all the way around. They're nutritious, inexpensive and versatile. I typically use dried beans, but the canned beans are good, too, and faster.

The Nantucket Pudding, which is pictured on page 126, is one of those things Mom always made, probably because it's fast. We had lots of blackberries growing up, all over the place, so that's what she used. If it's one thing I've learned over the years, it's to make the most of what you have on hand.

# *NAH's Favorite Meatloaf

*NAH is how our youngest son,
Neval Allen Harris, signed his name*

## Dinner

Sweet and Sour Meatloaf
*(Page 97)*

Yam and Potato Medallions
*(Page 104)*

Green Beans
with Bacon and Onions
*(Page 101)*

## Dessert

Pumpkin Pudding
*(Page 129)*

The topping on this Sweet and Sour Meatloaf provides a surprising mouthful of flavor and is a nice addition to the traditional meatloaf recipe.

Not all meatloaf variations I've tried over the years have been so well accepted.

The now infamous liver loaf is a good example.

Since we butchered our own meat, we had beef liver on hand. I love liver and onions. But no one else in the family was crazy about liver. You mention it and they make faces. They would eat it, but not without protest. I never understood the issue.

So one day, I thought I would use liver in a meatloaf, thinking they would not notice the switch. I parboiled it and ground it up. It looked like meatloaf.

Neval Allen, the youngest, who was about 12 at the time, loved meatloaf. It was one of his favorites and the rule at our house was if you put it on your plate, you had to eat it.

So, he loaded his plate with what he thought was meatloaf. Then he took a bite.

We negotiated the rule on that one occasion.

I never made it again.

Meatloaf continued to be a favorite of his, but he never failed to ask if liver was involved before digging in.

# Reba and Luke's Request

## Dinner

Rouladen
*(Page 89)*

Bread Dumplings
*(Page 99)*

Beets

**M**y grandson Luke stayed with us for a couple months when he was working in Leavenworth a few years ago. He and his sister Reba both nominated Rouladen as one of the favorites to include in the cookbook.

Several of the kids and grandkids have moved in and out of the house over the years, sometimes staying for extended periods of time, or just for a few days. That means we've never been complete empty nesters.

Mom lived downstairs until she passed away and my brother Jerry lives there now.

I'm cooking for just three or four of us these days, on a regular basis, depending on the day. But I feed anyone who shows up and looks hungry.

I got both the rouladen and dumpling recipes when I worked at a German restaurant in Leavenworth. In the restaurant, they had a bread chipper machine that transformed stale French bread into cubes for the dumplings.

**E**very family creates its own traditions, especially for holiday meals.

Those traditions evolve over time, as circumstances and the family dynamics change.

This Thanksgiving menu includes some of the dishes that have appeared pretty regularly on the table at our house over the years. Individually, each family member's "traditional" menu would probably be slightly different.

My kids might not consider Chard Bundles or Crab Puffs as traditional, since those items have been added in the past 20 years.

The grandkids never met Mrs. West (who was a neighbor here in Plain in the 1960s) and probably they don't remember her fruit salad recipe (which we haven't actually served in years), but their parents (at least those who were still at home when we shared the table with Mrs. West, Charlie and Tim) do and still consider it part of the tradition.

Food is an effective way to connect generations. Well, maybe it's not the food alone, but more the experience of working together to prepare the meal and then sitting down to eat and drink and share the stories of past get-togethers and, 'Do you remember the time when ...'

For our family, one of those stories is how we ended up in Plain.

## Plain

When World War II started, a lot of people from Eastern Washington moved to Seattle to work at Boeing or the shipyard. Several families from Plain who had kids my age moved into our Seattle neighborhood when I was about 12.

I stayed in touch with a couple of

**Light Supper**

Frittatas
*(Page 79)*

Bacon-Wrapped Grapes

Cantaloupe

the girls, and we wrote letters back and forth after the war ended and they returned to the eastern side of the mountains. So that's how I knew about Plain.

When I was on my own and wanted a different view of the state, I packed up the four kids (ranging in age from 4 to 14) and the dog into the yellow Dodge truck.

We moved into a cabin in Shugart Flats.

It had no electricity or running water. It had a wood stove and an outhouse.

It was my first outhouse.

I hated it. I always knew something was going to come out of that dark hole. And I refused to use it at night. I kept a coffee can in the house as a

I was about 14 when this photo was taken. Learning to cook was not anywhere on my "to do" list.

chamber pot.

One day while I was in there, a lizard jumped onto my bare thigh. I had never been around lizards like they have here. It gives you a start. That time I just screamed and brushed him off. I didn't have to go to the bathroom anymore.

The outhouse had a door of sorts, but it faced an open field with trees behind it and nobody was around, so you didn't need to bother with the door. After the lizard incident, I started leaving the door open, thinking it was better to have some light so I could see what might be lurking in the corners.

It was fine until one of the

I packed up the truck and four children — Tex (John), Bud (Charles), Mary and Bill — and moved to Plain in 1960 for a fresh start. I married a logger and we added two more to the family – Nevonne and Little Neval.

neighbors rode by on his horse.

"Good afternoon," he said.

When your pants are down around your ankles and you jump up to grab the door … you fall on

# Sausage Pepper Bake
# with Cheesy Polenta

## Dinner
Sausage Pepper Bake
*(Page 90)*

Cheesy Polenta
*(Page 90)*

Green Beans

## Dessert
Banana Cream Cake
*(Page 111)*

your face and whatever modesty you were trying to preserve is lost.

The neighbor got an eyeful and a story to tell.

By the time I arrived in Plain, I knew the basics of how to cook, but was about to learn a lot more. We arrived at the end of July. It was hot, but when all you have is a wood stove, you use it if you want to cook.

The first lesson was how to adjust the flue so it doesn't smoke. It's not hard to learn. And you learn how to cut and split wood, though I was already familiar with that.

Without an ice box or any kind of refrigerator, we ate everything fresh. You cook just enough beans for one meal.

We lived in the cabin for a year, or so, through one winter.

During that time, I met and later married Neval Harris, who was a logger. His brother Lorn lived in Shugart Flats then, as did his Aunt Dolly. We moved into the old Telford place, which had electricity and running water. No more outhouse.

I learned more about everything in the next few years. The people here were all farmers. They knew how to do it all and were happy to pass on the information. By then I was willing to ask for advice.

After moving to Plain, I married Neval Harris, who grew up here. He was a logger by trade. We eventually moved onto the property his grandparents and mother had purchased in the 1930s.

I learned a lot from Laura Burgess – how to make sauerkraut, how to garden. She was funny and she was a good cook, but I was never in that kitchen when the cupboard doors were shut. I don't think she ever closed the drawers. Ever. She was one of a kind.

We soon added two more to the family, Nevonne and Little Neval (who we called Tiny), and then moved onto the home place, where we still live.

## Roast Beef Dinner

Herbed Tip Roast
*(Page 81)*

Horseradish Sauce
*(Page 81)*

Mashed Potatoes and Gravy

Brussels Sprouts

We joined two cabins, one built by his grandparents (Charles and Martha Richards) and the one Neval had grown up in with his mother, Lizzy, and his brothers Elmer, Lorn, Tom and Charles. We painted it red with yellow trim.

My Dad put in the plumbing, so we had a bathroom and running water, which came from a spring that would usually go dry in February. We would take 50-gallon drums to the neighbors and fill them up.

That red cabin (of the Red Cabin Cookbook) later housed the Plain Bakery. By then we had built a basement foundation and moved the old Shugart house (which we bought from Bill and Trinna Burgess) onto it. That white house is featured on the cover of this book (The painting of the house was a gift from Grandson Adam).

We had cows (for milk and beef), chickens, pigs and a big garden. I canned everything — meat, soup, vegetables, fruit. I never used much processed frozen food until the last 15 years. I either had fresh or canned.

Lizzie Harris and the boys moved to Plain in 1936 from Number Two Canyon in Wenatchee. The move was made in a wagon pulled by a horse and a mule. Back row, from left: Tom, Lizzie and Charles. Front row: Lorn, Neval and Elmer.

Things have changed.

I can't garden like I used to. Now I just have berries — strawberries, blackberries and blueberries.

Friends and neighbors share produce from their gardens these days. And Neval's nephew Tom, who has large garden in Malaga, keeps us well-supplied with squash, corn, cucumbers and tomatoes.

I buy everything else. We probably have more variety now than when I was cooking for a

## German Go-To Theme

### Dinner

Schnitzel
*(Page 91)*

Potato Pancakes
*(Page 104)*

Applesauce

Brussels Sprouts

Schnitzel and potato pancakes were popular offerings when I worked at the German restaurant in Leavenworth. Note the menu doesn't include dessert. The Germans typically have their desserts as an afternoon snack with coffee (similar to English tea) rather than as an after-dinner sweet. And most of the desserts they do have are not as full of sugar as those we are used to here at home.

family of eight. Then we ate only what we could grow.

I canned a lot. Fruit, whatever we could get — peaches, pears, plums, cherries, apricots. And applesauce, plus jam. And then vegetables — green beans, beets, squash, Swiss chard, corn, tomatoes (and tomato sauce). I canned relishes, dill pickles, bread and butter pickles. I canned beef vegetable soup, pea soup, chili. When we killed chickens, I canned chicken.

We bought potatoes from Albert and Goetze, who lived down River Road. They raised potatoes.

And we had a milk cow, so we made butter and cottage cheese.

I put up more than 300 quarts of fruit, vegetables and tomatoes every year. I canned as much as I had or could get.

In this dinner photo, Mary prepares to blow out the candles on the cake for her 10th birthday. Pictured, clockwise, from left, Mary, Bud, Nevonne, Bill, me, Neval, Al (neighbor), Tex, Helen and Buck. Al's wife, Vi, took the photo.

One year, it frosted early and I had lots of little green cherry tomatoes. Instead of throwing them away, I pickled them, using the same brine as I did for dill pickles. They were pretty good.

The kids thought they looked like goat eyes, so when they had company over for dinner, they made a big deal about daring their friends to try a goat eye. When you bit into it, it would squirt clear across the table, creating some additional drama for those who accepted the dare.

I also put up pickled crab apples, which are sweet and spicy, great for Christmas. And I would add food coloring to the pears, to make some red and some green for Christmas and Easter. They're really good with cottage cheese.

Of course, I'm only cooking for three of us on a regular basis now, unless we have a family dinner, which happens quite a bit, between holidays, birthdays and other special occasions.

# Taco Theme

## Appetizer
Guacamole Dip and Chips
Chili Dip and Chips
*(Page 36)*

## Dinner
Taco-Flavored Chicken Wings
*(Page 98)*

Taco Salad
*(Page 45)*

Fruit Plate

## Dessert
Whoopie Pies
*(Page 134)*

*Over the River ...*

## Special Guests

*(Uncle Jerry's favorite)*

### Appetizer

Ham and Cheese
Wheels
*(Page 38)*

### Dinner

Crab-Stuffed
Chicken Breast
*(Page 76)*

Orange Rice
*(Page 103)*

Asparagus

Marinated Tomatoes
*(Page 101)*

### Dessert

Nantucket Pudding
*(Page 126)*

**C**rab-stuffed chicken breast was a favorite when I worked at the mountain lodge. The food there was advertised as "Country Gourmet."

I hadn't eaten out much in restaurants and didn't know what was being served, so when I got the job, I started looking at magazines to get ideas and the owners would provide some input. They wanted something that looked impressive.

It was fun to come up with recipes using ingredients you normally don't get to use every day when you're cooking for the family. And at home, you don't always take the time with presentation.

The owners would order the main ingredients, the meat and dry goods. Then I would stop at Dan's Market on the way in to pick up the fresh ingredients.

We provided dinner for 15 to 20 adults who would stay for up to a week at a time, with a set menu, though we tried to accommodate anyone with allergies.

They had a wine hour before dinner, so we made hors d'oeuvres for that.

I had a free hand and could make whatever I wanted. The kitchen door was always open and guests would come and stand at the door and watch and often ask for the recipes.

I made fresh bread every day — short loaves of braided bread for individual servings — and homemade noodles.

It was a very laid-back atmosphere. I never had a complaint.

In the summer, you could drive up to the lodge, but in the winter, you had to ride the snowmobile up and down. And there were no lights. It's a narrow road that drops straight down on one side.

They had a snow cat for the guests. If I had heavy things that couldn't fit on the snowmobile, I would send them up on the snow cat. If the timing was right, occasionally I would ride up in the snow cat and then ride the snowmobile back down.

It was a learning experience for a 60-something.

## Coffee Break

Eclairs
*(Page 120)*

Apple Kuchen
*(Page 109)*

Blueberry Cookies
*(Page 132)*

Lemon Squares
*(Page 124)*

Dried Fruit Bars
*(Page 119)*

**W**e've never skimped on sugar. My husband has a sweet tooth. Always has had one. He has some kind of dessert every day, sometimes more than one.

When he was working, the loggers would stop here on their way home and get a treat and coffee or beer.

I would bake almost every day. But I was a stay-at-home mom then. It was fun to cook for them because they never turned anything down.

And I still always try to have something on the counter, either cookies or cake or something for anyone who wants it. We still have quite a few guys who pass through. That's the first place they look.

Not too long ago, I made rhubarb pie and one of the guys who was here for dinner had to leave before we made it to dessert, so I cut into the pie and sent a piece home with him. When I dished it up for the rest of us, I soon realized I had forgotten the sugar. It happens.

A week later, I saw the fellow who had left early and I asked him, "How was that rhubarb pie?"

He said, "Man, it was good. It was pretty tart, but I ate it all."

They don't usually complain.

# Mother's Day Dinner

## Dessert
Cheesecake
(Page 113)

## Dinner
Cornish Game Hens with Black Cherry
Sauce (Page 75)
Rice with Butter and Soy Sauce
Asparagus
Spinach Salad

# Waiting for Santa

## Appetizers
Roasted Nuts
Chips and Dip

## Dinner
Baked Ham

Potato Salad
*(Page 44)*

Green Salad

Homemade Bread
*(Page 50)*

## Dessert
Cookies
*(Page 117)*
Pie
Candies
*(Page 140)*
Stollen
*(Page 66-67)*

W̲e always have the same thing for our Christmas Eve celebration, a buffet dinner with ham and potato salad. The side dishes and appetizers vary. And we have cookies and candies.

I used to make two kinds of candy for Christmas —hand-dipped chocolates (Page 140), a recipe I got from Betty Carveth, and then caramel squares (Page 140). Years ago, I made divinity as well. Back in the early days, when Albert and Goetze were still around, everyone would gather at the Grange Hall to make candy

Nevonne inspects the Christmas Eve dinner spread before Santa arrived — Christmas 1963. Note the potato salad, even back then.

canes.

We open our presents on Christmas Eve rather than Christmas Day, something we started when the kids were small.

It just made more sense. When you have a big family, the kids don't want to go to bed early, and you have everything to do to get ready for Christmas Day and it's just exhausting. So we have the big buffet dinner on Christmas Eve and eat leftovers on Christmas Day.

When the kids were little, they would plan an after-dinner program, with Christmas carols or songs they learned at Sunday School. Every year while they were in their bedrooms getting ready, Santa would arrive.

He is very clever.

# Turkey Patties

## Dinner

Turkey Sausage Patties
*(Page 98)*

Mashed Yams
*(Page 101)*

Mom's Spinach
*(Page 102)*

## Dessert

Fruit Bowl — honeydew melon and blueberries, or fruit in season

My mom, Lila Turner Vey, loved this spinach recipe. She fixed it all the time. She got it from her mother (Big Grandma), who grew up in Kansas.

# Party Food Fun or Wine Time

**M**ost of the get-togethers we have now are holidays, birthdays or some other family occasion. And most of those are potluck events.

We have hosted a few bigger bashes over the years that were well-attended by friends and neighbors. When Big Neval was still logging, one hot summer we had a log-rolling party. We put a couple of peeled logs in the pond and the competitors (some wearing their cork boots) would face off and try to stay upright.

After the party, one of the logs was left in the pond, getting waterlogged on one side, so it was a lot easier to stand on, but still good balance practice. The kids used it as a raft for a couple of years.

We also had some smaller get-togethers that started as wine tasting parties and turned into kitchen dances, with some family members using brooms as partners (which eliminates the danger of stepping on toes).

# Pork Chops
# and Pineapple

## Appetizer
Bacon-Wrapped Water
Chestnuts
*(Page 36)*

## Dinner
Pork Chops with Glazed
Pineapple Rings
*(Page 85)*

Spanish-Style Quinoa
*(Page 94)*

Broccoli

# Family Night

## Appetizer
Crab Puffs
*(Page 37)*

## Dinner
Pork Loin
with Mustard Marinade
*(Page 87)*

Confetti Bean Salad
*(Page 41)*

Broccoli

## Dessert
Rhubarb Pudding Cake
*(Page 130)*

# Sunday Brunch

Strata
*(Page 95)*

Orange Scones
*(Page 65)*

Pastries
*(Page 62)*

Watermelon and Blueberries

Sparkling Cider or
Champagne

## Leftover Surprise

### Dinner

Shepherd's Pie
with Turkey
*(Page 92)*

Marinated
Tomatoes
*(Page 101)*

### Dessert

Chocolate
Pudding Cake
*(Page 115)*

I **can't** get over being a squirrel. I always put away food for the winter.

We live 15 miles from town. I couldn't always get to the store every week. It might be two weeks or a month between trips, especially in the winter.

And I never knew how many people would show up for dinner on any given night. We often have visitors — friends and neighbors — who stop by and stay for dinner.

Making a meal on the fly when unexpected guests arrive is easier with a well-stocked pantry. It also helps stretch your food budget.

For years I made menus, which saves money and helps with nutrition since you can see what the family is eating or is not eating and come up with ways to create a more balanced diet.

Here are some dollar-stretching ideas to help keep your budget balanced and save time:

## MEALS ON A BUDGET

Make menus for two weeks at a time and shop to the menu, substituting items if you find something unexpected on sale.

### Plan for leftovers

Make a main dish meat — roast or turkey — on Sunday. Use the leftovers to make other items later in the week.

**Leg of Lamb** (page 86) becomes lamb and lentil stew (Page 48). Serve with pita bread and green salad.

**Roast Turkey and Stuffing** (Page 88) becomes filling for homemade flour wraps (Page 60); shepherd's pie (Page 92) and turkey soup (Page 49) with homemade egg noodles (Page 139).

**Baked Ham Dinner** on Sunday becomes frittatas (Page 79) and fruit on Monday and a freezer full of split pea soup (Page 49) to enjoy in the weeks to come.

Buy beef and pork roasts when the price is right. They can be divided into several cuts for later use – roast, steak, stir fry.

### Mashed potatoes

Use leftover mashed potatoes to make tuna or salmon fritters or a variation of shepherd's pie. It might be worth making some extra mashed potatoes for use later.

**Fritters:** Mix mashed potatoes with a can of tuna fish, season with diced onion, green onion or onion powder. Put in refrigerator for an hour to make it easier to handle.

Wet hands and form patties. Dip in egg and cracker crumbs (you can use flour) and fry.

Serve with vegetable (green beans with bacon and onion)

**New Bride's Tasty Beef Casserole:** Fry hamburger (or any ground meat) and diced onions. Add a can of tomatoes or tomato sauce and a can of drained green beans. Pour into a greased casserole dish. Top with mashed potatoes and bake until heated through. You can top potatoes with grated cheese or sprinkle with paprika for color.

# PANTRY PICKINGS

## Cornbread and chili

Make a large pan of cornbread (Page 55), freeze in family serving-sized bags. Serve with a can of chili and cheese. Or canned sausage gravy.

## Pasta and sauce

**Pasta Alfredo:** Mix cooked pasta, canned Alfredo sauce with Parmesan cheese for a fast meal that can be stretched to feed an unexpected crowd.

Add ingredients to suit. Mushrooms, vegetables. You can add meat, too. It turns into something more elegant with shrimp, cod or fillet of salmon.

**Slungoulian\*:** Sauté onion, pepper and celery until soft. Add a can of diced tomatoes, season to taste (oregano, basil, pepper and garlic powder).

Turn to low and simmer. Mix with cooked pasta, add Parmesan cheese.

You could add hamburger, sausage, Spam, etc., whatever you have on hand.

Serve with French bread.

(*Anytime Mom made a casserole, Dad called it Slungoulian)

## Bratwurst and sauerkraut

I try to keep bratwurst in the freezer and a can of sauerkraut on the shelf. We like it and it's quick to fix.

Sauerkraut actually goes with quite a few things. For those who aren't a fan, try the sour bratwurst

## Full pantry (prepared for any raid)

### PANTRY STOCK

Chili (with or without beans)
Jalapeño chilis
Green chilis
Spam
Tuna fish
Shrimp
Alfredo sauce
Diced tomatoes
Tomato sauce
Parmesan cheese
Mushrooms
Olives
Sauerkraut
Green beans
Bread crumbs
Egg noodles
Pasta, variety
Coffee
Cocktail sauce
Canned and dried beans: variety
Canned fruit
Applesauce

Canned milk
Crackers, variety
Panko crumbs
Graham crackers
Taco chips
Waxed paper
Foil
Parchment paper

### BAKING BASICS

Flour (whole wheat and white)
Sugar
Cocoa
Brown sugar
Sugar
Yeast
Molasses
Oatmeal
Baking soda
Baking powder
Salt
Shortening
Olive Oil

### FREEZER STOCK

Pies
Cake layers
Cookies
Cinnamon rolls
Bran muffins
Brownies
Scones
Biscuits
Corn bread
Bread
Baked potato boats

### REFRIGERATOR STOCK

Milk
Butter
Cream cheese
Sour cream
Buttermilk
Cottage cheese
Cheddar cheese

(Page 94) and cabbage (Page 99).

## Starts & snacks

**Chili dip** (*for chips, crackers or vegetables*): 1 can of hot chili with beans, 1 small can of jalapeño chili peppers, cumin, cream cheese.

Mix all together in a food processor. If it's too thick, add some sour cream.

Refrigerate until ready to serve.

**Shrimp dip:** Whip a package of cream cheese. Form into a mound and pour cocktail sauce over the top, cover with canned shrimp (well-drained). Serve with crackers.

## Beverages

**Cambridge Tea:** Heat equal parts water and canned milk, add

See pages 139, 142 and 143 for more hints.

sugar and garnish with nutmeg. This is a good alternative to hot chocolate.

**Milk and molasses:** Mix a couple tablespoons of molasses in milk for an afternoon break.

## Time savers

• Use rue balls to thicken sauces. You can keep the balls in a plastic bag in the freezer and use as needed.)

Take 5 tablespoons butter and 2 heaping tablespoons flour and mix together into a paste. Form them into 1-inch balls. Freeze. Use as needed.

• Mix sugar and cinnamon together and keep in the cupboard for sprinkling on everything from pies you're baking to slices of buttered toast in the morning.

# Appetizers

## Bacon-Wrapped Water Chestnuts

Bacon-wrapped anything is good. The chestnuts provide a satisfying crunch, but you can also use grapes or cantaloupe. Or put cream cheese in a jalapeño or sweet pepper and wrap with bacon. They disappear pretty quickly.

Use 1/2 slice bacon and one water chestnut for each hors d'oeuvre. Wrap bacon around the water chestnut and hold in place with a toothpick.

Put on baking sheet (foil-lined for easy clean up) and bake 30 minutes at 350 degrees.

## Brie in Puff Pastry

| 1 sheet frozen puff pastry
| 1 wheel Brie
| 1 egg, beaten

Thaw pastry sheet enough so you can unfold it. On a floured board, roll it out so it's large enough to fold over the Brie wheel. If desired, trim off a strip to use as decoration on top.

Fold pastry sheet over Brie, brushing edges with egg to help seal. Brush top with egg wash.

Add decorative strip in shape of bow or flower. Brush with egg. Place on parchment-covered baking sheet.

Bake in a 400-degree oven for 25 minutes. Serve with crackers.

## Chili Dip

| 1 14-ounce can of chili
|   with beans
| 4 ounces cream cheese
|   or 1 cup sour cream, or
|   a mixture of the two

| 1 small can chopped
|   chilis or 2 T. finely
|   chopped green pepper
|   (or red, yellow or orange
|   pepper)
| 1 t. cumin

Mix well. (A food processor works great.) Use sour cream to thin if necessary.

Serve with tortilla chips.

# Crab Puffs

*These filled mini cream puffs look difficult at first glance, but they sure come in handy when you're on the hook for a contribution to a party or potluck.*

## Puff Shells

- 1/2 cup water
- 1/4 cup butter or margarine
- Dash of salt
- 1/2 cup flour
- 2 eggs

Combine water, butter and salt in saucepan; bring to boil. Add flour all at once and stir vigorously until mixture forms a ball and leaves the side of the pan (if flour is lumpy at all, might want to sift first). Remove from heat.

Add eggs, one at a time, beating thoroughly after each one. Continue beating until a stiff dough is formed. Drop by level teaspoons onto a well-greased cookie sheet (I cover with foil and spray with Pam. Parchment paper also works, though make sure it's not hanging over the side of the pan to reduce flame potential).

Bake in a 450-degree oven for 10 minutes. Reduce heat to 350 degrees and bake another 10 minutes or so. Yield about 55 puffs.

When cool, cut in half and fill with whatever … crab, tuna or chicken salad are all good. Or pudding or … the sky is the limit.

*HINT: It's a challenge to get 55. If you don't get quite that many, it's OK, though maybe add a few minutes to the baking time.*

## Crab filling

- 8 oz. cream cheese
- Crab (I use the imitation crab. Whatever size package you can find.)
- Lemon juice
- Horseradish
- Onion powder
- **Optional:** 1/3 to 1/2 cup mayonnaise or sour cream

With a mixer, whip the cream cheese, then add the crab. You want it to break up into little pieces, but not be pulverized. Add a splash of lemon juice, a couple of teaspoons of horseradish and some onion powder to taste. Sometimes more lemon is good. You don't want it soupy, though.

If you want to make it go farther or make it lighter, you can add mayonnaise or sour cream, about a half cup or so for each package of cream cheese. Again, to your taste. You can just do cream cheese and crab and nothing else if that's all you have available.

This is also good in a wrap or on a toasted English muffin, in case you have any left over.

# Deviled Eggs

8 hard-boiled eggs,
  cooled
1/2 cup mayonnaise
1 T. mustard (add 1 T.
  curry powder, wasabi
  or hot chili sauce for
  variety)
Paprika to garnish

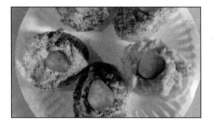

Peel eggs. Cut in half and put yolks in a bowl and whites on a plate or serving dish. Mash yolks with a fork. Add mayonnaise and mustard and mix well. Fill center of whites with yolk mixture. Sprinkle top with paprika.
  Chill until ready to serve.

# Ham & Cheese Wheels

*These appetizers look good and can be made ahead of time.*

Cream cheese
Green onions (or
  asparagus)
Ham slices (thin enough
  to roll)

Soften and whip cream cheese to spreading consistency. Blot dry the ham slices.
  Spread cream cheese to cover ham slice. Lay onions or asparagus along long edge. Roll ham slice as tight as possible. Chill at least an hour. Slice into wheels.

# Salmon Ball

1 large can salmon,
  drained
1/2 t. liquid smoke
1 T. horseradish
1 T. lemon juice
1 8-ounce package of
  cream cheese
2 T. mayonnaise
1 T. parsley

Mix well, form into a ball, log or shape suitable for the occasion. Roll in chopped nuts and parsley. Garnish with parsley and paprika.

# Shrimp Dip

1 8-ounce package
   cream cheese (at room
   temperature)
Cocktail sauce
1 can shrimp, drained

Whip cream cheese, form into suitable shape. Cover with cocktail sauce and top with shrimp.

Serve with crackers.

# Spinach Dip

10-ounce bag frozen
   chopped spinach
8-ounce package of
   cream cheese
1 cup sour cream
1 T. onion powder
Salt and pepper

Boil chopped spinach for 3 minutes. Drain well (Squeeze and blot to get rid of as much moisture as possible).

Whip cream cheese, add seasoning and sour cream and then spinach. Chill in covered container until ready to serve.

# Stuffed Mushrooms
### (Low carb version)

1 pound white button,
   cremini or portabello
   mushrooms (uniform
   size)
1 pound ground sausage
   (spicy or regular)
5 green onions, chopped
1 cup grated cheese
1 egg
Seasoning to taste
   (pepper flakes, basil,
   etc.)

Remove stems from mushroom caps and chop finely. Place caps (bottom side up) on foil-covered baking sheet.

In a frying pan, brown sausage (break into small pieces). Add onions, mushroom stems. Cook until soft. Cool. Mix in egg and cheese.

Spoon filling on each mushroom cap.

Bake 375 degrees for 20 minutes — or so, depending on size of mushrooms.

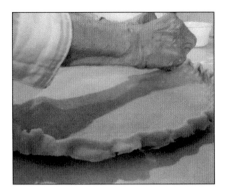  

# Zwiebelkuchen

## (Onion tart)

*This German tart is traditionally served with new wine. But everything goes with beer, at least some people think so. We also like it as a main course for a brunch, with green salad and fruit.*

1 pie crust
6 slices bacon, cut small
3 onions, chopped
3 eggs, beaten
3/4 cup sour cream
1/2 t. salt
1/8 t. pepper
1 T. chives
1/2 t. caraway seeds

Roll out pie crust to fit a 13-inch round pizza pan. Crimp up edges to prevent the filling from escaping. Bake 10 minutes at 375 degrees.

Fry bacon over medium heat. Remove bacon from pan. Sauté onions in bacon fat until soft. Combine eggs, sour cream, salt, pepper and chives. Add bacon and onion to egg mixture, pour into pie shell. Sprinkle with caraway seeds. Bake for 30 minutes in preheated 375-degree oven.

Serve hot or cold.

# Salads

## Cherry Applesauce Jell-O Salad

1/2 cup Red Hots (hard cinnamon candies)
1 cup boiling water
1 package cherry Jell-O
1 can applesauce
8-ounce package cream cheese
1/2 cup mayonnaise
1 1/2 T. sugar
1/2 cup celery, chopped
1/2 cup pecans, chopped

Dissolve candies in boiling water. Add Jell-O, stir until dissolved. Stir in applesauce. Pour half the Jell-O mixture in bowl or mold, chill until firm.

Mix together softened cream cheese, mayonnaise and sugar. Beat well. Add celery and pecans. Spread cream cheese mixture over firm Jell-O layer. Top with remaining Jell-O mixture. Chill.

## Confetti Bean Salad

*This is a good summer-time salad. You could add cubes of ham to make it a complete meal.*

1-pound bag of navy beans, cooked with 1 t. soda, and cooled
1/3 cup oil
2 T. lemon juice
3/4 cup sugar
1 t. salt
1/2 t. pepper
3/4 cup cider vinegar
1/2 cup each green pepper and red pepper, chopped
3 green onions, chopped
1 T. chopped cilantro
1 cup of sharp cheddar cheese, cubed
Green olives with pimentos (optional)

Mix oil, lemon juice and vinegar. Add sugar and spices, stir until sugar is dissolved. Add peppers, onions, cilantro and cheese (and any other add-ins). Fold into beans. Put in bowl with tight cover and refrigerate, stirring every couple of hours, until time to serve.

**HINT:** *It tastes better the second day.*

**HINT 2:** *This is the same basic recipe as Four-Bean Salad. Rather than navy beans, substitute 1 can each of drained green beans, yellow wax beans, red kidney beans and garbanzo beans.*

# German Potato Salad

7 medium yellow potatoes
3 green onions, sliced
2 T. parsley, chopped
4 slices bacon, chopped
1/2 cup each cider
  vinegar and olive oil
1/2 t. each salt and
  pepper (or to taste)

Boil potatoes with skins on. Cool to room temperature. Cut into bite-size chunks.

Slice and fry bacon. Cool slightly. Mix bacon, bacon grease, onions and parsley with potatoes.

Mix vinegar and oil and add to potato mixture. Season to taste.

Serve at room temperature.

# Lentil Salad

1/2-pound dry lentils
  (green or brown)
3 T. red wine or cider
  vinegar
2 T. oil
1/2 t. salt
Pepper
1 clove garlic, chopped
1/2 medium onion,
  chopped
1/2 cup green onion,
  chopped

Drop lentils into 3 cups boiling water. Reduce heat and simmer, partly covered for 30 minutes (until tender, but not mushy). Cool and drain under cold water.

Once cool and well-drained add other ingredients and let marinate at room temperature for 1 hour, stirring every 15 minutes.

Chill.

# Pasta Salad

2 cups uncooked pasta,
  cooked and drained
3/4 cup mayonnaise
2 T. mustard
2 dill pickles, chopped
3 hard-boiled eggs sliced
1/2 cup sliced olives
  (green or black)
3 green onions, chopped

1/2 cup cubed cheddar
  cheese (optional)
1 cup cubed ham (or
  summer sausage or
  cooked bacon)
Salt and pepper to taste

Mix all together. Garnish with parsley, paprika. Chill until ready to serve.

# Salad Dressings

## Blue Cheese Dressing

    4 cups buttermilk
    1 quart mayonnaise
    1/2 T. garlic salt
    2 t. prepared mustard
    1 cup blue cheese or
       Roquefort cheese

Mix all except cheese. Whip until smooth. Crumble and add cheese. Store in refrigerator (in a jar with a tight lid). If the dressing is too thick after sitting, thin with buttermilk.

This is also good on baked potatoes or pasta.

## French Dressing

    1 medium onion
    1/2 cup vinegar
    1/2 cup ketchup
    1 1/2 t. salt

Blend for 1 minute (in blender or food processor). Add 1 cup sugar. Add 1 cup oil, slowly, until well blended. Makes 3 cups.

## Sour Cream Dressing

    1 cup sour cream
    2 T. vinegar
    1 T. lemon juice
    1/8 t. cayenne pepper
    1 T. sugar
    1 t. salt

Combine and mix well.

## Broccoli Salad Dressing

    1 t. powdered mustard
    1 T. mayo
    2 T. vinegar
    Salt and pepper to taste

Cook broccoli flowerets until tender (don't overcook). Drain and cool. Chill.

Mix dressing and broccoli. Serve on shredded lettuce. Sprinkle with chopped walnuts. (Serves 4)

## Sour Cream Rosemary Dressing

    1 t. dried rosemary
    3 T. hot water
    Steep 5 minutes. Strain
       and add:
    1 cup sour cream
    1 cup mayonnaise
    2 green onions (chopped
       fine)
    1/4 t. salt
    2-3 T. vinegar

Good on spinach salad.

## Cheese and Herb Dressing

    4 cups mayonnaise
    1 cup parsley, chopped
    1 cup Parmesan cheese
    8 t. lemon juice
    4 cloves minced garlic
    4 t. fresh basil
    Buttermilk (as needed)

Mix first six ingredients until well blended. Thin to suit with buttermilk.

## Italian Salad Dressing

    2/3 cup oil
    1/3 cup wine vinegar
    1/2 t. salt
    Dark pepper
    1/4 t. garlic powder
    1 T. oregano

Shake all together. Chill. Shake before using.

## Italian Sweet and Sour Dressing

    1/2 cup oil
    1/2 cup vinegar
    2 T. sugar
    1/2 t. salt
    1/2 t. celery salt
    1/2 t. pepper
    1/2 t. dry mustard
    1/2 t. Worcestershire
       sauce
    1/4 t. Tabasco sauce
    1 clove minced garlic
    1/2 t. garlic powder

Put in jar and shake. Makes 1 cup.

Add to 2 1/2 quarts spinach, chopped or torn, 1 1/2 cup quartered mushrooms. Garnish with red pepper.

# Pea Salad

1 10-ounce package frozen peas

1 can sliced water chestnuts

1 cup chopped celery

1/2 cup green onions, chopped

1/4 cup mayonnaise

1/4 cup sour cream

1/2 t. seasoning salt or salt and pepper

**OPTIONAL:** 3 hard-boiled eggs, sliced

Put frozen peas in boiling water, boil for 3 minutes. Drain. Put in ice water to cool. Drain well.

Add other ingredients, mix well.

# Potato Salad

*This is a perennial family favorite, requested for birthdays and other family gatherings. It has become a must-have for Christmas Eve dinner. We usually make a big batch and serve it in the shape of a tree. It's always good for a late-night snack. And it's even better the next day.*

5 medium potatoes

Green onions, chopped

Olives and dill pickles, chopped

5 slices of bacon, chopped

3 boiled eggs

3/4 cup mayonnaise

Mustard

Salt and pepper to taste

2 T. parsley (fresh or dried)

Boil potatoes with the skins on. Drain, cool and peel.

Fry bacon (better to cook it slowly, which renders the fat and makes it not too crispy).

Chop onions, olives, dill pickles. Mix with cut up potatoes. Add cooked bacon and bacon grease. Add a splash of vinegar or pickle juice.

Add mayonnaise and mustard, mix well. Add sliced boiled eggs and parsley. Mix well. Salt and pepper to taste. Garnish for the occasion.

Refrigerate.

# Sweet and Sour Zucchini Salad

4 slices bacon, chopped small, sautéed and drained (reserve the grease)
1 T. bacon grease
2 T. flour
Cook and add:
2/3 cup red wine vinegar
1 1/3 cup water
1/2 t. pepper
1 t. salt
4 T. sugar
9 cups shredded zucchini
Sliced mushrooms and tomatoes (for garnish)

Sauté bacon. Set aside.

In sauce pan combine bacon grease and flour, stir. Add remaining ingredients and cook until thickened. Add bacon. Cool.

Just before serving, mix with zucchini.

Serve on mounded lettuce greens and garnish with mushroom and tomato slices.

# Taco Salad

1 large head of lettuce
1 cup chopped tomatoes
1/2 cup black olives, sliced
1/2 cup green pepper, chopped
1 cup grated cheese (cheddar or jack)
1/2 cup chopped onion (or green onion)
1/3 cup cilantro, chopped
1-pound chub of spicy sausage, browned and cooled.
1 cup crushed Doritos

Toss all together. Serve with sour cream and salsa or mix ranch dressing and salsa.

# Soups

## Bean & Kale Soup

2 pounds beans (1 pound
   each red beans and
   navy beans)
Ham scraps
1 1/2 cups chopped
   carrots
1 onion, chopped
3 cloves garlic, chopped
2 cups tomatoes (fresh or
   canned) - or handful of
   dried tomatoes.
1 pound kale, chopped.
Salt and pepper to taste.

Soak beans overnight in water or cover with water and boil 10 minutes. Let sit for one hour, drain.

Cover soaked beans with water, add ham, vegetables and seasoning. Boil until beans are tender. If no ham scraps are available, use chicken or turkey. (You also could use chicken or beef broth rather than water)

Add more liquid if needed.

## Black Bean Soup

1 gallon water
1 1/2 cups black beans
   (soaked overnight
   in 2 quarts of water)
1 pound bacon, chopped
1 t. dried, crushed red
   pepper flakes

Salt and pepper
2 cloves garlic
Pinch of oregano
2 medium onions, chopped
2 cups celery, chopped
1 T. prepared mustard
Parsley

Simmer beans in water for five hours. Add other ingredients and simmer for another two hours.

This freezes well.

Pots of fresh herbs on the back porch make for easy garnish and salad additions.

# Gazpacho

3 cloves garlic
1/4 cup green pepper
1/4 cup onion or two
  green onions
1 cucumber
1 large tomato
8-ounce can tomato juice
1/4 t. cumin

Chop garlic, onion, green pepper, cucumber and tomato very fine. Set aside.

In a blender, mix tomato juice and cumin. Season to taste. Mix blended liquid with finely chopped vegetables.

Serve with flour tortillas topped with melted cheese.

# Hamburger Soup

*Like many soups, this is versatile, allowing you to use almost any vegetable. The challenge is it's never the same twice, but always good. It also freezes well if you have leftovers.*

*I serve it with bread, crackers or cornbread, depending on who I'm feeding and how hungry they are. Some of the people I feed eat a lot.*

1 pound hamburger
1 large onion
2 stalks celery
4 large carrots
1 large can chopped tomatoes
4 medium potatoes or 3/4 cup
  barley (This can be left out
  for those low-carbers.)
6 cups water
Salt and pepper to taste
1 bay leaf

In a soup pot, brown hamburger (use oil if using lean meat). Add water, tomatoes and other chopped vegetables. Bring to a boil, reduce heat and simmer, covered, for an hour.

Season to taste … salt and pepper, garlic or boullion.

*Over the River …*

# Lamb & Lentil Stew

*If you have leftover roasted lamb or leg of lamb, this is a good way to use it. Boil the leftover lamb bone until tender. Take meat off bone. Reserve liquid. This is also good with barley rather than the lentils.*

Cooked lamb, chopped
1 cup carrots, chopped
1/2 cup green or red
    peppers, chopped
2 cups dry lentils
1 1/2 cups diced
    tomatoes (or a
    15-ounce can)
2 quarts liquid (reserved
    from boiling the bone, or
    other soup stock)
Salt and pepper to taste
2 t. fresh thyme
1 T. oregano

Simmer lentils until soft. Add carrots, green pepper and lamb. Simmer until tender. Season to taste (and depending on how much seasoning had been used on the ham.

Serve with pita bread and salad.

Leg of Lamb for one meal can be stretched to a second meal by boiling the bone for soup or stew.

# Navy Bean Soup

2 cups navy beans
3 cups cold water
A chunk of ham or
    sausage
1/2 cup chopped celery
1/2 cup chopped carrots
1 medium onion, chopped
1/2 cup barley

Soak beans in water overnight. Drain the beans and add fresh water to cover beans, plus 1 inch.

Add meat, vegetables and barley.

Bring to a boil, then turn down to simmer until beans are soft. Season with salt and pepper to taste. Thin with water if necessary.

# Plain Vegetable Soup

1 quart tomatoes
1 large onion, chopped
2 stalks celery, chopped
1 can or pint of green
    beans
1 quart boiling water

Put all into a pot and cook gently for 30 minutes. Season with salt and pepper and add a handful of rice, macaroni or broken spaghetti. Cook gently 30 minutes more.

# Potato Soup with Bacon

1/2 pound bacon, cut into 1/2-inch pieces
1 cup yellow onions, chopped
3 pounds red potatoes, cubed (about 4 cups)
1/4 pound margarine (1 cube)
1 quart cream, canned milk or milk
Salt and pepper to taste

Put bacon, onions and potatoes in a large pot, with enough water to cover. Bring to a boil. Reduce heat to simmer and cook until potatoes are mushy (about 30 minutes). Add more water if necessary.

Add margarine and cream (or milk). Season to taste.

If mixture is not thick enough, make a paste of cornstarch and water and stir into simmering mixture, stirring until thick.

Garnish with chopped parsley. Serve with biscuits, crackers or crusty bread.

# Split Pea Soup with Smoked Pig Knuckles

2 smoked pig knuckles (or ham bone or bacon)
2 pounds split peas
2 T. onion powder (or to taste)
1 cup diced carrots
Salt and pepper to taste

Boil knuckles in 3 quarts of water, simmer until tender. Add split peas, onion powder and carrots.

Add more water as needed.

Cover, simmer on low until peas are soft, stirring occasionally to keep from sticking to the bottom.

Salt and pepper to taste (depending on how salty the meat).

You can use chicken stock or bouillon if you prefer.

# Tom Turkey Soup (or Chicken)
### *with Homemade Egg Noodles*

1 turkey carcass
1 yellow onion, chopped
2 carrots, chopped
2 stalks celery, chopped
1 batch of homemade egg noodles (or choice of pasta, barley or other grain)

Break up carcass and put in soup pot. Add enough water to cover, bring to a boil, simmer covered until meat is falling off the bones (about 2 hours).

Remove the carcass and any loose bones. Set aside until it's cool enough to get to the meat. Pick it clean, returning meat to the pot. (At this point, you can freeze it for later, if you don't want to make the soup now.)

Add chopped vegetables. Return to a boil. Add salt and pepper to taste. Drop in homemade egg noodles (See recipe, page 136) and boil for 20 minutes.

# Breads

## White Bread

8 cups warm water
3 packages yeast
1/2 cup oil
1/2 cup sugar
1 cup dry powdered milk
3 T. salt
White flour

Put all the ingredients except for the flour in a large bowl and stir will. Add enough flour, a cup at a time, to make a batter than can be beaten with spoon. Beat well. Cover with a towel and let sit for 5 minutes. Add flour, a cup at a time, and stir after each addition.

When you have a stiff dough, turn out onto a floured surface and knead for 10 to 15 minutes.

Put in greased bowl and cover. Raise until double in size.

Punch down and divide into six loaves. Pans should be two-thirds full.

Raise until double and bake in a 375-degree oven for 35 minutes.

## Egg Bread

Make the same as for white bread except add 4 eggs when you have the dough thick enough to beat. Beat well after adding each egg, then continue to follow white bread recipe directions.

Before putting pans in oven, brush with milk and sprinkle with sesame seeds.

The dough also can be used to make sandwich buns or you can braid the loaf and bake on a cookie sheet.

This freezes well.

# Things you should know about bread baking

- Try to have your ingredients at room temperature. Do not put your dough into a cold bowl to raise or into cold pans.
- Oil, margarine, butter, lard, bacon grease can all be substituted for each other.
- Sugar, molasses, honey and even jams and jelly can be substituted for each other.
- Salt and sugar are in bread to make the yeast work better, as well as for flavor. They can be left out if, for some reason, you can't eat them. The same goes for oil. It can be left out. You can make a pretty decent loaf of break with just water, yeast and flour.
- Leftover cooked cereal, wheat germ, sieved vegetables, fruit, eggs — almost anything edible — can be added to bread recipes. Keep in mind, though, that the extra ingredients are going to add to the raising time.
- The only really 100-percent whole wheat flour is graham flour.
- Add flour a little at a time. Try to keep the dough soft without being sticky.
- If you raise your bread in the oven — with the oven light on and a pan of hot water on the bottom shelf — you don't need to cover the dough while it's raising. I always raise mine like this. Of course, keep the door shut.
- Grease the dough on top when raising to keep it from drying out.
- Unless you like a dry hard crust, oil the tops of the loaves when they come out of the oven.

- You can bake bread in any kind of pan.
- Any bread recipe can be cut in half.
- The first raising is the most important. Be sure you raise the dough until it is at least double in size.
- If, after the second raising, you have to wait for any reason, punch it down and re-raise. But always keep the dough from getting cold.
- Hot liquid will kill the yeast. Liquid should be pleasantly warm.
- After punching down your dough and getting ready to form into loaves, if you find it is not easy to work with, cover it and let it sit for 15 minutes. It will be easier to handle.
- Remove the loaves from the pans and let them cool on racks or on their side on a cloth. If left in the pan to cool, they will get soggy.
- To test the doneness of a loaf, turn out and thump the bottom of the loaf with your knuckle. If it sounds hollow, it's done.
- It takes longer to toast homemade bread than it does commercial bread. If your slices won't fit in the toaster, put it under the broiler.
- To test yeast dough to see if it has risen enough, punch the center of the dough with two fingers. If the dough is sufficiently raised, the holes will not fill back in. If they fill in quickly, raise a little longer.
- When making French bread, slash the top before baking to keep the crust from breaking.

# Whole Wheat Bread

8 cups warm water
4 envelopes dry yeast
1/2 cup molasses
1/2 cup oil
3 T. salt
Whole wheat flour

In a large bowl, put the water, molasses and yeast. Let stand for 5 minutes. Add oil, salt and enough flour to make a batter thick enough to beat. Beat thoroughly. Add flour, a cup at a time, until you can't stir it with a spoon. Dump onto floured surface and knead until smooth. Place in a greased bowl and raise until double in size. Punch down and divide into loaves.

Place in greased pans (pans should be half full), and raise again until double in size. Bake in a 375-degree oven for 30 minutes, turn down oven to 350 degrees and bake for another 15 minutes. Remove to racks and grease tops.

# Light Wheat Bread

8 cups hot water
1 cube margarine
3 packages dry yeast
1 large can of canned
   milk
1/2 cup molasses
3 T. salt
6 cups whole wheat flour
White flour

Stir margarine into hot water until melted. Cool to lukewarm. Add yeast, milk, salt and 4 cups of whole wheat flour. Stir well and stir in 2 more cups of flour — one cup at a time. Beat well. Add white flour, 1 cup at a time, until dough is thick. Turn out onto a floured surface. Knead at least 10 minutes.

Raise in a greased bowl, covered, until double in size. Punch down.

Divide into loaves and place in greased pans. Raise until double and bake in a 375-degree oven for 40 minutes.

# Sandwich Buns

Use any of the bread dough recipes — or the cinnamon roll dough. After raising the first time, punch down and let stand 10 minutes. Divide dough into balls, whatever size you want, but make sure they're all the same size. Place on a greased cookie sheet (several inches apart so they don't touch). Let stand for 10 minutes, then flatten to form a bun shape (about 3/4-inch thick).

Cover and let raise for 30 minutes.

Bake in 360-degree oven for 20 minutes.

# Frau Sturm's Bayern Brot

## *Farmers Bread*

This recipe is from Frau Sturm, the owner of a gasthaus in a small village in Germany. She sent it to me via my son, John, who was a regular customer.

This bread is very heavy, but good. I splurge on some real butter to eat with this bread. It is good for open-faced sandwiches as well.

I make it with part rye meal and part rye flour, as the German rye flour ground locally there is coarser than what we have available in stores here. I also have made this bread with whole wheat with good results.

You will probably want to slice it thin. And it freezes well. I usually quarter the loaf and freeze part of it.

Below is the recipe, just as Frau Sturm sent it to me.

Also included is the sourdough starter, which takes a week before it is ready and, like any sourdough starter, you want to save some for the next batch. If you have sourdough that you use regularly, you can use it instead. You will need 1 cup of starter.

> # Glaze for Dark Breads
>
> 1 ounce corn starch
> 1 pint water
> 1/4 ounce salt
> Bring to a boil. Brush on bread as soon as it comes out of the oven.

### The Sourdough Starter:

    2 cups warm water
    2 cups rye flour

Mix together in a glass bowl with a wooden spoon (never let sourdough come in contact with metal).

Put in a glass or crock-type container and sit in a warm place for five days.

### The Bread:

The night before you plan to bake bread, mix 1 cup of sourdough starter with 1 1/2 liters of lukewarm water. Let sit overnight, covered, in a warm place.

(I put mine in the oven, with the light on, covered with a dish cloth.)

In the morning add a pinch of salt and fold in enough rye flour to form a dough, but do not knead.

Let sit, covered, in a warm place for four hours.

After the four hours, knead it until you have a smooth, fine dough. Form into a large round loaf that is 2 inches high and 12 inches to 15 inches in diameter. Wet your hands and rub over the outside of the loaf to smooth the skin. Place on a greased baking sheet. Let rise in oven (Place a pan of hot water on the bottom shelf) for one hour.

Bake at 400 degrees for 1 1/2 hours.

# Butterflake Loaf or Rolls

*This is a different way to make loaves or rolls that adds a special touch to meals where soup or stew is the main course.*

Use egg bread dough, which has been raised once and is ready to form into loaves.

Roll dough into a 4-inch-by-12-inch rectangles, about 1/2-inch thick.

Cut it into four pieces (each 4-by-3-inches).

Brush both sides of each piece with melted butter. Stand them up (with the 4-inch side across) in a lightly oiled loaf pan, adding pieces until pan is full.

Allow to raise until double.

Bake in a 350-degree oven for 30 minutes.

• To make rolls, use a lightly greased cupcake pan, cut dough pieces slightly smaller (2-by-2-inches), brush with butter, layer.

Raise, bake in a 375-degree oven about 20 minutes (timing could vary depending on size of layers).

# Buttermilk Biscuits

*Biscuits are quick, easy and versatile, working well when unexpected company comes and you need to stretch the meal. The dough also can be used for quick cinnamon rolls for Sunday breakfast, or as the topping for a casserole with meat, vegetables and gravy.*

2 cups flour
1 T. sugar
2 1/2 t. baking powder
1/2 t. salt
1/4 t. soda
3/4 cup buttermilk
1/3 cup oil

Mix dry ingredients in a bowl. Make a hollow in the center and pour in buttermilk and oil.

Mix only until flour is wet. Turn out on board with some flour and gently fold over about five times. Form a round and flatten it to 3/4-inch thick. Cut with biscuit cutter or cookie cutter (or wedges).

Bake in preheated 425-degree oven for 15 minutes.

If the biscuits are touching, they will get taller, but might take a little longer to bake.

## *Quick Cinnamon Rolls*

Roll the biscuit dough into a square. Spread dough with softened butter or margarine, sprinkle with cinnamon and sugar.

Add raisins or chopped nuts if desired, but not necessary.

Roll up, pinch edge to seal. Cut slices about 1-inch thick. Place on lightly greased baking pan. Bake in 425-degree oven for 18 minutes.

Mix together 1 cup powdered sugar and a little milk and drizzle over rolls when still hot.

# Buttermilk Cornbread

1/2 cup melted butter
2/3 cup sugar
2 eggs
1 cup buttermilk
1/2 t. baking soda
1 cup cornmeal
1 cup flour
1/2 t. salt

Stir sugar into melted butter. Add eggs and beat until well blended. Combine buttermilk with baking soda and stir into mixture in pan. Stir in cornmeal, flour and salt until well blended. Pour batter into greased pan (8-inch pan for smaller recipe).

Bake in preheated 375 degree oven for 30 to 40 minutes (until toothpick comes out clean).

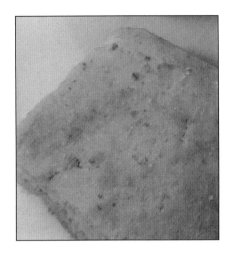

# Buttermilk Pancakes

*Great for breakfast and brunch. We have these for dinner, too, maybe once a week.*

2 cups flour
1/2 t. salt
1 1/2 t. soda
1 t. sugar
2 cups buttermilk
2 T. melted butter or oil
2 eggs
Blueberries, bananas or berries, if desired.

Beat eggs, milk and oil together. Blend dry ingredients and add to egg and milk mixture. Blend until mixed well. If it's too thick, add water.

Heat frying pan. Pour pancake batter, adding fruit as desired. Turn when bubbles stop filling in.

# Casserole Breads

### Egg Casserole Bread

- 5 1/2 to 6 1/2 cups flour
- 2 T. sugar
- 1 T. salt
- 2 packages of dry yeast
- 2 T. soft butter
- 2 cups warm water
- 3 eggs (room temperature)

Beat together 1 1/2 cups flour and all other ingredients except eggs.

Beat 2 minutes. Beat in eggs and work in remaining flour until a soft dough is formed.

Let it stand for 35 minutes. Stir down and pour into two greased 1 1/2-quart casserole plans. Let rise until double. Bake in a 375-degree oven for 35 to 45 minutes.

### Poppy Seed Batter Bread

- 1 1/4 cup water
- 1 package yeast
- 2 T. soft butter
- 2 T. poppy seeds
- 2 T. sugar
- 2 t. salt
- 3 to 3 1/2 cups flour

Mix together to form a batter. Let raise. Put in greased casserole or bread loaf pan. Let rise.

Bake for 45 minutes in a 375-degree oven.

### Cornmeal Onion Batter Bread

- 1 cup yellow cornmeal
- 1 1/4 t. salt
- 2 t. baking powder
- 2 cups milk
- 2 eggs
- 1/2 cup chopped green onion
- 1 cup boiling water
- 2 T. oil

Combine cornmeal, salt and baking powder in a greased 1 1/2-quart casserole. Stir in milk, eggs and onion and beat well with whisk. Stir in water and oil and mix well.

Bake in preheated 375-degree oven for 35 minutes or until puffed and golden brown.

Serve immediately.

Makes six servings.

# Crackers

**Whole Wheat Snacking Crackers**

- 2 cups whole wheat flour
- 1 t. salt
- 1/2 cup wheat germ
- 1/2 cup sesame seeds
- 1/2 cup oil
- 1/2 cup cold water

Blend together flour, salt, wheat germ and sesame seeds. Sprinkle oil over and mix well with a fork. Pour water over and mix well. (You may have to add a little more water, but don't get too moist.)

Knead for at least 10 minutes. Pull off golf ball-sized pieces, roll into a ball and, with a rolling pin, roll into a 5-inch circle.

Cook in iron skillet (turning until light brown on each side) or bake in a 400-degree oven for about 6 minutes.

**Variations:** Replace 1 cup whole wheat flour with same amount of cornmeal, rye flour, oats or buckwheat. Rather than sesame seeds, use poppy seeds, soy grits, shredded coconut or ground nuts.

You can also add seasonings: Thyme, sage, rosemary, marjoram, chives, dill, savory, basil, garlic, caraway or Parmesan cheese.

**Rye Crackers**

- 1 cup rye flour
- 1 cup whole wheat or white flour
- 1/2 t. salt
- 1/2 cup water
- 5 T. oil

Mix dry ingredients. With a fork, stir in water and oil. Knead 10 minutes. Make into balls the size of walnuts and roll paper thin on a floured board. Place on ungreased cookie sheets and bake at 425 degrees for 8 minutes.

**Baking Powder Crackers**

- 2 cups white flour
- 1 T. baking powder
- 1 t. salt
- 1/2 cup milk
- 5 T. oil

Mix dry ingredients in a bowl. Add milk and oil, store with a fork until well blended. On a lightly floured board, knead about 10 times. Form into balls about the size of walnuts and roll paper thing. Sprinkle tops with water and top with sesame seeds or poppy seeds. Place on ungreased cookie sheets and bake in 425-degree oven for 8 minutes or until golden brown.

# Cinnamon Rolls

*(made from sweet dough)*

*This is a recipe that I've used for cinnamon rolls and other sweet rolls. This is the dough we used in the Plain Bakery.*

2 cans evaporated milk
2 cups boiling water
4 packages dry yeast
2 cups sugar
1 1/2 t. salt
2 cubes margarine,
   melted
3 eggs
Flour

**Filling:**

1 cup melted margarine
   or butter
1/2 cup cinnamon
2 cups brown sugar
1 cup white sugar
1 cup raisins and
   chopped walnuts
   (optional)

**Topping:**

Glaze of powdered sugar,
   milk and vanilla. Mix to
   suit.

Pour the milk and water in a large bowl. Cool to lukewarm and add yeast and sugar. Stir.

Add enough flour to make a dough about as thick as cake batter. Cover and set aside for 15 minutes.

Beat eggs. Add eggs and salt to the dough. Beat well. Add melted margarine, mix. Start adding flour, 1 cup at a time, stirring after each addition. Don't put so much flour in at a time that the dough is too stiff.

Dump out on a floured surface and knead for 10 minutes. Put dough in a greased bowl, cover with cloth and keep in warm place. Allow to raise until doubled. (Placing it in a warmed oven, with a pan of hot water works well. It will take at least an hour.)

When it has raised enough, dump onto a lightly floured surface and knead for 3 minutes. Put back in bowl and let sit for 10 minutes.

Roll into 3/4-inch thick rectangle. Spread with butter or margarine. Add raisins and nuts (if desired). Sprinkle with cinnamon and sugar.

Roll up like a jelly roll, pinching edges to seal. Cut into 1-inch-thick slices. Place on greased cookie sheet, leaving 1 inch between each roll. Press down lightly on each roll so they touch. Cover and raise in a warm place for 30 minutes.

Bake in a 350-degree oven for 35 minutes.

Remove from oven, grease tops with margarine while still warm. Move from pan to wire rack to cool.

Drizzle powdered sugar glaze over rolls (though they are good without, too).

## Dinner Rolls

Pinch off golf-ball-sized pieces of dough, form into balls, place in greased baking pans. Raise for 30 minutes and bake in 400 degree oven for 20 minutes.

## Ham & Cheese Rolls

Rather than the cinnamon and sugar filling ... blend together chopped ham,

grated cheese and mustard. Roll up and slice the same way as for cinnamon rolls. Bake. Serve warm or cold.

# Flour Wraps

  4 cups flour
  1 T. baking powder
  1 1/2 t. salt
  1/2 cup shortening
  1 cup water

Place flour, salt and baking powder in bowl. Cut in shortening. Add water and stir to moisten, until it can be kneaded. Knead for 5 minutes.

Place in warm, covered bowl and let sit for 90 minutes.

Divide into 2-inch balls. Roll each ball to about 8 inches in diameter, making the rounds are an even thickness.

Cook on hot griddle or skillet for 1 minute each side. They will puff up and brown.

Stack on foil to cool. Wrap and freeze.

# German Onion Cake

*This "cake" is a savory batter bread that is wonderful served with soup or stew, fried chicken, ribs or sausage. A variation of the Zwiebelkuchen (Page 40), the Germans serve it with new wine.*

**Dough:**
- 2 cups flour
- 1/4 cup corn starch
- 4 t. baking powder
- 1/4 t. salt
- 5 T. shortening
- 1 cup milk

**Topping:**
- 2 cups chopped onions
- 2 T. butter
- 1/2 t. salt
- 1/2 t. pepper
- 1/2 t. marjoram
- 1 egg
- 3/4 cup sour cream
- Paprika

Mix dry ingredients. Cut in shortening. Add milk (enough to make a batter).

Pour batter into greased and floured 9-inch cake pan.

Sauté chopped onions in butter with salt, pepper and marjoram. Spread over dough.

Mix egg and sour cream, pour over onions. Sprinkle with paprika and poppy seeds.

Bake for 20 minutes in a 450-degree oven.

# Irish Soda Bread

- 4 cups flour
- 3/4 cup sugar
- 1 t. salt
- 1 t. soda
- 1 1/2 t. baking powder
- 1/4 cup butter
- 1 egg, beaten
- 1 1/2 cups buttermilk
- 1 T. caraway seed
- 3/4 cup raisins
  (Optional)

Sift dry ingredients. Cut in butter. Add raisins and caraway seeds.

Beat together buttermilk and egg. Add to flour and mix, knead (adding flour if necessary) until it forms a ball.

Flatten until it's about 3-inches thick.

Place on lightly greased baking sheet, cut an X in the top.

Bake at 350 degrees for 1 hour.

# Pastries

*I found the original recipe for these pastries in the Mother Earth News magazine about 30 years ago. Van Camp's Bakery in Seattle (whose brand logo was blue with wind mills) had similar pastries.*
*Makes 6 pastries (each serves 1-4, depending on appetite)*

**Pastries**

- 2 envelopes yeast
- 3/4 cup warm water
- 1 T. sugar
- 1/2 cup sugar
- 1/2 cup butter or margarine
- 1 cup sour cream
- 4 eggs *(2 in dough and 2 for egg wash)*
- 1 1/2 t. salt
- 1/2 t. nutmeg
- 1 T. orange zest
- 6 cups flour
- Filling of choice *(Bavarian cream, raspberry, cream cheese are favorites). It takes about 3/4 cup for each pastry.*

**Streusel topping:**

- 2/3 cup sugar
- 2/3 cup flour
- 1/3 cup butter or margarine
- 2 t. cinnamon

**Icing:**

- 2 cups powdered sugar
- 1 T. warm water or milk
- 1 t. oil
- 1/4 t. vanilla

Mix together yeast, water and sugar in a small bowl and let stand for 10 minutes.

Add sugar, butter, sour cream, 2 eggs, salt, nutmeg and orange zest. Mix well. Add flour (2 cups at a time), mixing well between additions. Knead until dough is smooth (it will still be a little tacky, but not sloppy).

Put in greased, warm bowl and cover. Let raise until double in size. (About an hour)

Divide into six balls. Shape each into 4-inch squares, cover and let

 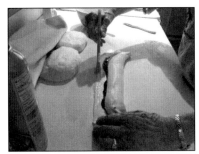  

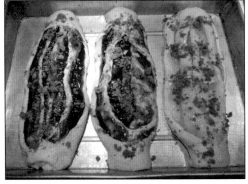

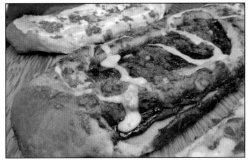

sit for 20 minutes. (That will make it easier to roll out, though it's easier said than done. I grease the counter, my hands and the rolling pin)

Roll each into 10-inch squares.

Spread filling (about 3/4 cup) to within 1/2-inch of edge. Brush egg wash (2 eggs beaten with 1 T. water) on edges, roll tightly, sealing ends.

Put on greased baking pan, seam side down. Take a sharp knife and cut through two layers of dough, spread to form oval shape. Brush with egg wash and sprinkle with streusel topping.

Cover and let raise until double (about 45 minutes).

Bake 350 degrees for 20 to 25 minutes.

Take out of pan and put on cooling rack immediately (or it will stick). Drizzle with icing.

**SHAPE OPTIONS:**

• Slice the roll diagonally and fan out the layers.

• Fold dough over filling once, seal and then slice through the top layer to reveal filling.

• Put filling down the middle and slice the edges and braid over the top.

• Make smaller pastries, build up sides and fill in a single layer.

*Over the River ...*

# Pita Bread

2 3/4 cups lukewarm
  water
2 packages dry yeast
Pinch of sugar
8 cups flour
2 t. salt
1/4 cup oil
1 cup cornmeal or flour

Pour 1/4 cup warm water in a small bowl an sprinkle with yeast an sugar.

Let sit for 5 minutes. Combine flour, salt and 2 cups lukewarm water, oil and yeast mixture. Mix and add 1/2 cup more warm water to form a soft dough.

Knead 20 minutes.

Let raise 45 minutes. Form into eight balls. Let rest 30 minutes. Sprinkle cookie sheets with cornmeal.

Roll balls to 1/8-inch thick (about 8inches in diameter). Raise 30 minutes. Bake in 500-degree oven for 5 minutes. (They will puff up and brown slightly.)

# Pizza Crust

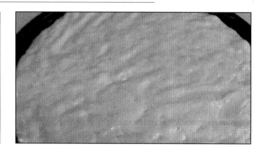

1 package dry yeast
1 cup warm water
2 cups flour
2 l. oil
2 t. sugar

Mix yeast, water and sugar and let stand for 5 minutes. Add oil and mix in flour to form a dough. Raise for 30 minutes. Spread onto greased pizza pan. Add toppings of choice.

Bake 350 degrees for 20 minutes.

# Potato Biscuits

1 package yeast
1/2 cup hot milk
2 T. oil
2 T. sugar
1/2 cup warmed mashed
  potatoes
1 t. salt
3 1/4 cups flour

Mix ingredients. Let sit covered in a warm place for 40 minutes. Roll and cut as for regular biscuits.

Bake for 20 minutes in a 400-degree oven.

# Scones

*These scones have an orange glaze to put on top. You could make them without the glaze and add 1/2 cup currants or blueberries (fresh, frozen or dried).*

2 cups flour
1/2 cup sugar
1 1/2 t. cream of tartar
3/4 t. baking soda
1 t. salt
1/2 cup butter or
   margarine, softened
1 egg
1 cup buttermilk (more or
   less as needed)
1 egg yolk
Sugar

Sift together dry ingredients. Cut in butter. Add whole egg and enough buttermilk to make a soft dough. Mix and turn onto floured board. Knead a few times, then roll to 1/2-inch thick round. Cut into wedges. Put on cookie sheet.

Beat egg yolk with a little cold water and brush on top of each scone. Sprinkle with sugar.

Bake in preheated 425-degree oven for 15 minutes.

While the scones are baking, make the orange glaze.

**Glaze**

1/4 cup margarine
1/3 cup sugar
Juice and zest of an orange (about 1/3 cup of juice
   and 2 T. zest)

Bring to a boil and then simmer for 5 minutes or so, stirring constantly.

Brush the glaze on the scones, let cool.

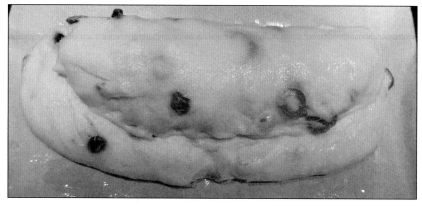

# Stollen

*These Christmas loaves make great gifts. They don't have to be just for the holidays, though. I love it for breakfast anytime.*

1 package yeast
1/4 cup warm water
1/2 cup milk
4 T. sugar
1 t. salt
2 T. butter, melted
3 cups flour
1 egg, beaten
1/4 cup chopped nuts
1/4 cup citron, candied cherries or dried cherries
1/2 t. lemon extract
1/2 t. cinnamon

Dissolve yeast in water, add milk, sugar, salt, melted butter, egg, lemon extract and cinnamon. Mix in enough flour to form a soft dough. Add fruit and nuts, knead in the rest of the flour, knead until smooth (about 10 minutes). Place in a greased bowl and cover. Allow to raise until double. Punch it down and raise again.

Form 1 large or two smaller oval free form loaves. Place on a greased baking sheet (or on parchment paper). Raise until double.

Bake in a 350-degree oven for about 30 minutes. Cool on a rack.

When cool, sift powdered sugar on top. This is especially great sliced thin and toasted with butter.

Wait to add the powdered sugar if you are planning to freeze.

# Sourdough Hot Cakes

**Sourdough Starter**
- 2 cups thick, warm potato water
- 2 T. sugar
- 2 cups flour

Put all ingredients in a glass bowl. Beat until smooth and creamy, cover with cloth. Place in a warm place for five days until it is sour smelling.

To make hot cakes:

The night before you want to make hot cakes, put your sourdough in a large bowl and add:
- 2 cups of warm water
- 2 1/2 cups flour
- 1 t. sugar

Beat well with a wooden spoon. (Never use metal bowls or spoons with sourdough.) Cover bowl with a cloth and put in a warm place overnight to raise. The oven, with the light on, is ideal. Next morning, reserve 1 cup of mixture and put in a jar, covered, in the refrigerator, for use next time.

To the remainder, add:
- 1 egg
- 2 T. oil
- 1/4 cup canned or dry instant milk

Beat together.

Combine:
- 1 t. salt
- 1 t. baking soda
- 2 T. sugar

Sprinkle over dough (Make sure the baking soda is lump-free). Fold into dough. It will foam up. Cook on lightly greased griddle. (Heat your griddle a little hotter than for regular hot cakes).

The next time you want to make hotcakes, use the sourdough you put in the refrigerator. Start at the beginning of the hot cake recipe and remember to reserve 1 cup of sourdough in the morning and you won't ever have to wait the five days again.

**O**ur garden is much smaller now than when we had six kids at home. We still enjoy berries, rhubarb and the flowers. The photos here were taken in the summer 2017, while son Bill spent his vacation watering and weeding.

*Over the River …*

# Main Dishes

## Bacon-Wrapped Burgerballs

1 pound ground beef or pork
1 egg
1/2 cup bread crumbs
2 T. chopped onion or 1 T. onion powder
2 cloves garlic, chopped or 1 T. powdered garlic
1/2 cup salsa or ketchup
Blue cheese chunks (or any kind of cheese – gorgonzola, feta, cheddar or smoked gouda)
1 whole medium-sized onion
2 slices bacon for each meatball

Mix ground meat, egg, bread crumbs, spices and salsa (ketchup). Form into uniform-shaped balls about 2 inches in diameter, with a chunk of cheese in the center.

Cut ends off the onion and cut in half, lengthwise. Peel off layers. Cover meatball with onion layers.

Use the back of a butcher knife to stretch the bacon slices, making them thinner and more pliable. Wrap each of the balls with bacon (cover completely).

Place on a baking sheet. Bake 1 hour in a 350-degree oven.

*Variation:* *Wrap green pepper rings around the meatball instead of, or in addition to, the onion and bacon.*

# Baked Pork Chops

1 t. oil
1 cup Parmesan cheese
1 cup bread crumbs
1 t. pepper
1 t. garlic powder
4 pork chops

Combine first five ingredients and rub on both sides of pork chops. (Blot chops dry before trying to coat).

Place on baking pan coated with cooking spray.

Bake at 350 degrees for 40-45 minutes. Turn after 20 minutes.

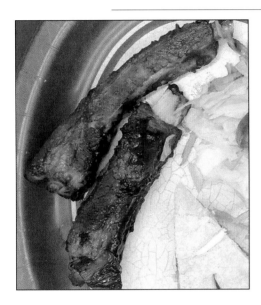

# Barbecue Ribs

Pork or beef ribs (about 4.5 pounds)
Barbecue sauce
*(Use a commercial brand or make your own by combining:*
*1 cup ketchup*
*3 T. mustard*
*3 T. brown sugar, garlic and onion powder to taste)*

Cut ribs into serving-size pieces. Boil until tender (about 1 hour).

Drain well. Brush on sauce. Bake in 350-degree oven, uncovered, turning several times and brushing with more sauce after each turn. Continue until well-glazed.

# Chicken Cacciatore

2 frying chickens, cut into pieces
3 medium onions
2 pounds mushrooms
2 T. flour
1/2 cup cognac or wine
3 cups chicken broth
6 cups chopped fresh tomatoes
3 T. each chopped parsley and basil

Season the chicken pieces as desired. Heat oil in frying pan. Brown chicken pieces. Set aside.

In same pan, add butter or oil as needed and sauté vegetables. Add flour and stir to make rue. Add wine, broth and tomatoes.

Simmer for 10 minutes.

Add chicken, cover, simmer for 30 minutes (or until tender)

Remove chicken to warming platter. Heat up sauce and cook until reduced. Add parsley and basil.

Pour over chicken pieces.

Serve with pasta.

# Chili

1 pound hamburger (or any ground meat)
2 1/2 cups cooked or canned kidney beans
2 cups tomatoes, chopped (or 1 large can of diced tomatoes)
1 cup water
1 clove garlic, minced
1/4 t. garlic salt
1/2 cup chopped onion
1/2 t. cumin
1 T. chili powder (or more, to taste)

Brown hamburger in a large skillet. Add onion and cook until limp. Add all of the other ingredients and simmer until the flavors are well blended.

Garnish with sour cream.

Serve with corn bread.

## Options

**Chili-Mac:** Make an easy chili-mac by adding 1 cup of macaroni or other pasta noodles, simmer until pasta is done. Serve with sour cream and cheddar cheese sticks.

**Tamale Pie:** To the basic chili recipe, add 1 cup black olives, 1 cup canned corn (drained). Pour mixture into a greased casserole dish, and cover with cornmeal topping (stir together 2 eggs, 1 cup milk and 1 cup cornmeal).

Sprinkle with grated cheddar cheese. Bake uncovered in a 350-degree oven for 45 minutes.

# Clam Fritters

*Clam fritters are a quick-and-easy, from-the-pantry dish.*
*This recipe also could be made with tuna fish.*

1 1/2 cups minced clams
  with juice
1/4 cup flour
1/2 t. baking powder
1/2 t. salt
1 egg
1/2 c up chopped green
  onions or chives (or 1 T.
  onion powder)
Oil

Beat egg, mix in clams and juice. Mix dry ingredients, add to egg mixture and mix until moist.

Heat frying pan and oil on medium.

Place heaping tablespoons of clam mixture into pan, spreading to about 3 inches in diameter. Fry until golden brown, turn.

Serve with blue cheese dressing or ketchup.

# Cod with Peppers

*(This also is good with halibut, scallops or chicken)*

1 fillet of cod, cut in four pieces
1 quart total of diced onions and
  peppers (red, green, yellow and
  orange)
1 T. fresh rosemary leaves (chopped
  fine in food processor)
1/2 cup diced tomatoes
1/2 cup each of bread crumbs and
  flour, seasoned to taste
Olive oil
1/2 cup Parmesan cheese

Heat oil in frying pan. Dip cod in bread crumb/flour mix and brown. Place in 9x9-inch baking dish.

Sauté peppers, onions and rosemary until onions are soft. Pour over top of cod. Top with tomatoes. Put in 350-degree oven for 20 minutes. Sprinkle with cheese.

# Corned Beef with Mustard Glaze

1 corned beef
   brisket
2 bay leaves
2 1/2 T. Dijon
   mustard
1 t. horseradish
   sauce
1 t. olive oil

Cook corned beef according to directions (Simmer in water with spices and bay leaf until fork-tender. It will take a couple of hours.)

Remove from pot.

Whisk together mustard, horseradish sauce and olive oil. Brush onto brisket. Put in 350-degree oven for 15 to 20 minutes.

For those who want the full boiled dinner experience, cook cabbage, potatoes and carrots in the water while the brisket is in the oven.

# Cornish Game Hens

*with black cherry sauce*

(Serves 10)

5 Cornish game hens

**Marinade**

2 cups lemon juice

1 1/2 cups melted margarine

1/2 t. paprika

3 t. thyme

2 1/2 t. salt

2 1/2 t. garlic powder

1/2 t. pepper

**Black Cherry Sauce**

2 cups black cherries, canned, with juice

2 T. vinegar

2 T. fresh rosemary

1/2 cup port wine (or red wine)

2 T. cornstarch, mixed with water

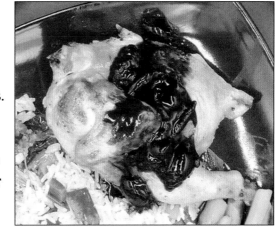

Cut hens in half, rinse, drain and blot dry.

Whisk together marinade ingredients. Reserve half for basting. Pour remainder over game hens and let stand for 30 minutes or longer. Put in roasting pan, skin side up. Bake at 375 degrees for 1 hour, basting with reserved sauce several times.

Remove from oven and cover with foil. Let stand for 15 minutes.

Combine cherries (with juice), vinegar and rosemary in saucepan. Simmer. Add wine. Add cornstarch dissolved in water. Stir over heat until it thickens (It will cling to the spoon).

Pour over hens or serve on the side.

# Crab-Stuffed Chicken Breasts
## *(with butter sauce)*

4 chicken breasts
8 ounces cream cheese,
   divided into four long
   slices
2 cups crab meat (1/2 cup
   for each breast)
8 T. horseradish sauce
   (2 T. each breast)
Pepper
1/4 cup butter

### Sauce

2 1-inch rue balls
1 cup chicken broth
1/2 cup sliced
   mushrooms, fresh or
   canned. *(Optional)*
Seasonings to taste
   (1/2 t. sage, basil,
   parsley, etc.)

### Rue Balls

*(Used to thicken sauces.
   You can keep the balls
   in a plastic bag in the
   freezer and use as
   needed.)*
5 T. butter
2 heaping tablespoons
   flour

Mix together into a paste and form into 1-inch balls.

Heat oven to 375 degrees.

Flatten boneless chicken breasts with the flat side of a meat mallet until about twice the size (about 1/3-inch thick). *(Tip: To prevent splatter, put breast in a plastic bag and pound through plastic.)*

Place flattened breasts skin side down. On each one, put a flattened slice of cream cheese, spread with horseradish and then top with crab chunks *(You could also mix together the cream cheese, horseradish and crab and divide stuffing between the number of chicken breasts to be prepared).*

Roll up each breast (fasten with toothpicks).

Put butter in baking dish (large enough to hold all four breasts without being too cramped) and place in oven long enough to melt the butter. Take pan from oven.

Roll top of stuffed breasts in butter in pan and then place seam-side down in pan.

Bake about 40 minutes, basting at least once with butter and juice from the pan. *(Time will vary depending on how thick the breasts are and individual ovens.)*

Just before chicken breasts are ready, make the butter sauce for the topping: Add rue balls, one at a time, to simmering chicken broth and seasonings — sage, basil, parsley, etc. Once thick, add mushrooms in desired. Pour sauce over finished chicken breasts and serve. You could add paprika if you would like to add more color.

## Serving suggestions:

*Serve with Orange Rice, fresh asparagus, marinated tomatoes and Nantucket pudding.*

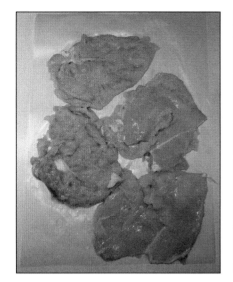

# Deviled Halibut Steak

2 T. prepared mustard
1 T. oil
2 T. horseradish
2 T. chili sauce
1 t. salt
4 halibut steaks

Mix mustard, oil, horseradish, chili sauce and salt. Brush half the sauce on top of the steaks. Broil on greased rack for 6 minutes. Turn, brush second side with remaining sauce. Broil 6 minutes more.

# Enchilada Bake

1 pound spicy sausage
(or could use any
ground meat)
2 packets taco seasoning
2 cups chopped sweet
peppers
2 cups water
1 T. granulated garlic
1 medium onion, chopped
1 small can (8 ounces)
tomato sauce
2 cups salsa
10 tortillas (flour or corn)
Grated cheese
Sour cream
Avocados (or guacamole)

Brown meat. Remove from pan. Sauté onions and peppers in olive oil until onions are transparent. Return meat to pan, add garlic and taco seasoning and water. Cover and simmer for 10 minutes. Add tomato sauce.

Spread half of the salsa in bottom of a 9x13-inch pan.

Put 1/2 cup meat filling on each of the tortilla shells, fold ends in and then fold over. Place seam side down in pan.

Mix juice from meat with remaining salsa and pour over the top of the filled enchiladas. Cover with grated cheese.

Bake in a 350-degree oven for 30 minutes.

Serve with sour cream and guacamole (or sliced avocados).

# Fish Alaska

2 cups mayonnaise
1 t. Dijon mustard
1 t. dill
6 salmon or halibut steaks

Mix mayonnaise, mustard and dill. Spread evenly on fish steaks. Bake in 425-degree oven for 10 minutes.

# Frittatas

1/2 pound bacon, chopped
1 cup each green onions, peppers, mushrooms and tomatoes (or other ingredients on hand — green olives, black olives, celery, zucchini, asparagus, potatoes)
1 T. granulated garlic
1 t. pepper
2 t. salt
1/3 cup milk
12 eggs
1/2 cup grated cheese (Parmesan, cheddar or pepper jack)

Brown onions, peppers and bacon in a large frying pan until the onions are done. Add other vegetables, sauté. Beat eggs and milk, salt, pepper and garlic. Pour into pan (don't stir). When bottom is brown, put pan in a 350-degree oven until the eggs are set.

Turn off oven, sprinkle with cheese and fresh basil. Let sit in oven until cheese is melted.

Serve with salsa.

# Glazed Chicken Wings

1/2 t. salt
1/2 t. garlic powder
1/4 t. pepper
1/2 cup brown sugar
1/2 t. cornstarch
1/4 cup vinegar

2 T. ketchup
1/2 cup chicken stock
1 T. soy sauce
3-5 pounds of chicken wings (fresh or frozen)

Combine all ingredients and pour over chicken in a baking sheet with 1-inch sides. Wings need to be in a single layer, so it might take two pans. Bake at 400 degrees for 35 to 45 minutes (until chicken is tender), turning every 10 to 15 minutes to glaze.

*Over the River ...*

# Grandma's Chicken

*(Fried chicken, baked with onions)*

1 frying chicken, cut into pieces *(You can also use boneless chicken breasts or thighs if that's what you have in the freezer)*
Flour
Salt and pepper
Olive oil
Onions, sliced

Wash and pat dry the chicken pieces. Coat the chicken in a mix of flour, salt and pepper. Brown in olive oil.

Put pieces in a roasting pan or Dutch oven, top with sliced onions. Add salt and pepper on top. Cover. Put in 350-degree oven for 30 minutes. Remove cover and bake another 30 minutes to brown.

# Herbed Sirloin Tip Roast
## *(with horseradish sauce)*

3-pound sirloin tip roast
1 T. thyme
1 t. each garlic salt, rosemary leaves, pepper and sage
Mustard or horseradish sauce

Preheat oven to 500 degrees. Mix spices. Roll roast in mixture. Place roast on rack in greased roasting pan. Put in oven. Turn temperature to 350 degrees. Roast 30 minutes per pound (until internal temperature is 155 degrees).

Serve with horseradish sauce or mustard sauce.

# Horseradish Sauce

2 T. butter
2 T. flour
1 cup of half-and-half
1 tablespoon horseradish *(use more or less depending on how hot you want it)*
2 T. butter
1 T. capers *(optional)*

Stir together butter, flour and cream and cook for 1 minute. Add horseradish, butter and capers.

*For mustard sauce, substitute 1/4 cup Dijon mustard for horseradish.*

# Meatballs, Sauce and Pasta

## Meatballs

- 2 pounds ground meat (any combination will work, using beef, pork sausage, turkey or buffalo. We used beef and spicy pork sausage)
- 1 small onion, chopped
- 2 cloves garlic, chopped
- 1 egg
- 2 t. salt
- 2 t. pepper
- 1 T. dried basil (or 1/2 cup chopped fresh basil)
- 1 cup bread crumbs

Mix well. Form into 1 3/4-inch balls (golf ball size). Put on baking sheet and bake in 425-degree oven for 30 minutes. Turn after 15 minutes.

Makes about 2 dozen balls. (If you're using ground turkey or other lean meat, you might need to grease the pan first.)

## Sauce

- 1/2 cup oil
- 2-pound can tomato sauce (or 2 14.5-ounce cans)
- 2-pound can Italian diced tomatoes (or 1 quart chopped fresh tomatoes)
- 2 medium onions, chopped
- 3 large cloves garlic, chopped
- 2 cups red or green pepper, diced
- 1 cup fresh basil (or 2 T. dried basil or Italian seasoning)
- 1 T. oregano
- 2 T. salt
- 2 cups water (add more or less to suit)

Use a large pot with a cover that can go in the oven.

On top of the stove, heat oil, sauté garlic, onion and peppers about five minutes or until soft. Add tomatoes and spices, stir well. Bring to boil. Add meatballs. Reheat to boiling. Cover and put in 335-degree oven for 90 minutes.

# Oven-Baked Barbecue Ribs

4 pounds pork spareribs
2 cups onions, sliced
2 cups ketchup
2 cups water
4 t. salt
1/4 cup Worcestershire sauce
1/2 cup white vinegar
1/2 cup dark brown sugar
4 t. dry mustard

Preheat oven to 350 degrees.

Combine onions, ketchup, water, salt, Worcestershire sauce, vinegar, brown sugar and mustard in a bowl.

Divide ribs by cutting between the bones. Heat a lightly oiled skillet over medium-high heat. Add ribs in batches and brown.

Place ribs in single layer in two baking pans or casserole dishes. Pour half the sauce over the ribs. Reserve remainder for basting.

Bake ribs 3 hours. For first two hours, turn and baste meat every 20 minutes, using all the sauce. For last hour, continue turning and basting using sauce in the pan.

*Makes six servings.*

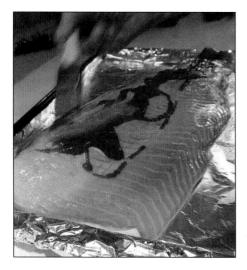  

# Paysanne Sauce (for fish)

1/2 cup green onions, chopped

1/2 cup green or red peppers, chopped

1 cup mushrooms, sliced

1/4 cup ketchup

2 T. melted butter

6 halibut or salmon steaks, 3/4-inch thick

Put fish on lightly greased baking pan.

Brush top of fish with ketchup, making sure to go clear to the edge.

Sauté onions, mushrooms and peppers in butter for 2-3 minutes.

Spread over ketchup on the fish.

Baking in preheated 375-degree oven for 15 to 20 minutes.

# Pork Chops with Glazed Pineapple Rings

Pork chops
Italian bread crumbs
Salt and pepper
Olive oil
Pineapple slices
Butter
Sugar

Dip pork chops in seasoned bread crumbs. Brown both sides in oiled frying pan. Put in 350-degree oven while preparing pineapple slices.

Sauté pineapple slices in butter. Sprinkle with sugar to help glaze. Put in oven on top of pork chops to finish cooking (about 15 minutes more).

# Pot Roast

1 pot roast (arm, blade, round, rump or chuck, 3 to 5 pounds)
Olive oil
3/4-cup water and beef boullion or beef broth
Salt and pepper to taste.
1 onion, chopped
3 large carrots (sliced or cut into sticks) or use smaller carrots, whole
2 stalks celery, cut in lengths

Pat the roast dry. In a pre-heated heavy skillet or Dutch oven, brown roast on both sides. Cover with chopped onions, carrots and celery. Add liquid, salt and pepper.

Cover with tight lid. Cook on low on top of the stove or put in 350-degree oven. Cook until tender (3 hours or longer, depending on how large the roast).

# Roast Chicken with Rice Stuffing

2 T. dried tomatoes (soak in water to soften)
1 cup cooked rice
4 basil leaves, chopped
2 green onions, chopped
1 1/2 T. butter
1 t. salt
1 t. pepper
1 T. parsley
1 roasting chicken

Sauté onions, spices and tomatoes in margarine. Mix with rice. Stuff chicken.

Bake 375 degrees for 1.5 hours (or until done, depending on size of chicken).

# Roast Leg of Lamb

6 cloves of garlic
Olive oil
Salt and pepper
Lamb (4.5 pounds, semi-boneless)

Peel garlic cloves and cut into slices. With a paring knife, make slits in meat and fill with garlic pieces.

Rub outside of meat with oil, sprinkle with salt and pepper. Put in roasting pan.

Put pan under broiler until brown on one side, turn, brown the other side.

Turn oven to 325 degrees. Put pan on middle rack, cover with a foil tent.

Roast until done — 130 degrees for rare or 135 to 140 degrees for medium.

Take out of oven, let sit, covered with foil, for 15 minutes. Slice and serve.

# Roast Pork Loin with Mustard Marinade

Pork tenderloin (about
  1-3/4 pounds)
**Mustard Marinade**
  1/4 cup Dijon mustard
  2 T. curry
  2 cloves minced garlic
  1/4 t. cinnamon

Mix marinade ingredients.

Blot pork tenderloin dry with paper towels, and roll in marinade. Put in a pan and cover (or in a plastic bag). Let sit in marinade in refrigerator for 4 to 24 hours.

Grease baking pan. Drizzle olive oil on loin (or put oil in pan and roll the loin in it.)

Bake at 325 degrees for about an hour (to 165 degrees). Slice and serve.

# Roast Turkey & Stuffing

1 turkey, thawed, with giblets and neck removed

**For the stuffing …**
1 cup each chopped onion and celery
1 cup chopped apples
1 cup walnuts
1 cube butter
1 T. salt
1 t. pepper
1 T. each oregano and sage
1/2 cup parsley (dried or fresh)
3/4 cup chicken broth
8 cups dried bread cubes (or 12- to 16-ounce package) for a 16-pound turkey. If you have a larger bird, double the recipe.

Sauté chopped onions and celery in butter until onions are transparent. Pour over bread cubes. Mix well. Fold in apples and walnuts. Add chicken broth and stir until mixed (moist but not sopping wet).

Rinse turkey and pat dry with paper towels. Put the stuffing in both ends (body and neck).

Place breast-side up in a roasting pan lined with enough foil to cover the bird. (*I criss-cross sheets of foil on the pan, leaving enough length on both sides and ends to meet and fold over on top.*) Fold the wings under the neck — which also helps hold the neck cavity stuffing in place. Rub the outside of the turkey with butter or oil. Add a cup of water inside the foil, then bring foil ends together and fold to seal. Place in the oven.

(*Follow the directions for time and temperature as printed on the wrapping. The rule of thumb for a stuffed turkey is 20 minutes per pound at 325 degrees, but it depends on weight and temperature and how tight you pack the stuffing. A meat thermometer is the way to go. According to the U.S. Department of Agriculture, the magic temperature is 165 degrees.*)

Open the foil and fold it down when you have about 30 minutes of roasting time left to allow the turkey to brown and crisp up the skin.

Remove from oven, bring foil back up to cover and allow the turkey to sit for about 15 minutes before carving.

Make gravy from the drippings. Use the giblets (heart and liver) and neck that have been boiled with celery and carrots.

# Rouladen

8 pieces of round steak, pounded 1/4-inch thick
Bacon slices
Pickle slices
1/2 cup sliced onion
1/4 cup spicy mustard
3 T. oil
1 1/4 cups water
2 cups beef broth

Spread each pounded steak with mustard. Place bacon, onion and pickle slice on top and roll up, securing the seam with toothpicks.

Brown in oil (over medium heat).

Place seam side down in baking pan. Add broth.

Bake in a 350-degree oven for 30 minutes.

Make gravy from drippings.

# Sausage & Pepper Bake with Cheesy Polenta

2 red peppers, sliced
2 green peppers, sliced
4 garlic cloves, chopped
2 t. dried oregano
1/4 t. crushed dried red pepper
2 T. olive oil
2 pounds sweet Italian sausage or
  bratwurst

Heat oven to 350 degrees. Combine vegetables and spices in a 13x9x2 inch baking dish. Pour oil over and mix well. (Season with salt and pepper to taste).

Brown sausages, turning often. Place on top of peppers in baking dish. Bake 45 minutes, stirring occasionally.

Serve with cheesy polenta.

# Cheesy Polenta

1 1/2 cup water
1 cup cornmeal (white or yellow)
2 1/3 cup chicken or vegetable broth
1 cup grated Parmesan cheese
1/4 cup milk or cream
2 T. butter

Combine water and cornmeal in a small bowl. Bring broth to a boil in a large saucepan.

Gradually add cornmeal mixture, stirring until well blended. Reduce heat to low and simmer, stirring occasionally, until thick (about 15 minutes).

Mix in 1/2 cup Parmesan cheese, milk and butter. Add salt and pepper to taste. Put in a serving bowl and sprinkle with remaining cheese.

# Schnitzel

Pork tenderloin, cut into 1/2-inch thick slices
1 1/2 cups flour, seasoned with salt and pepper
2 eggs, beaten with 1 T. water
2 cups bread crumbs or panko

Pound pork slices until they are about 1/8-inch thick, as even as possible.

Put flour, egg wash and bread crumbs into separate pans (pie tins work well).

Using a heavy frying pan on medium, heat 1/4-cup oil.

Dip pounded pork slices first into flour, then egg wash, then bread crumbs. Fry until golden brown.

All stoves are different, so it's difficult to say how long that will take, but keep a close eye as it's easy to get them too brown. Another method is to brown them in the frying pan and then put them on a cookie sheet in a 350-degree oven for about 15 minutes to finish cooking.

(If you are serving with Potato Pancakes, page 104, put them in a 325-degree oven while you make the pancakes.)

# Scrambled Eggs with Cream Cheese

6 eggs
2 T. butter
2 T. cream cheese

Whisk eggs in a small bowl. Heat butter in a frying pan over medium heat. Add eggs, stir until well mixed. Add cream cheese and continue stirring until eggs are almost set. Remove from heat, salt and pepper to taste.

Serve.

Don't over-cook.

# Shepherd's Pie

*(Great for roast turkey leftovers — or any leftover meat, for that matter)*

2 1/2 cups cooked turkey, cubed

1 cup each chopped onions, carrots, celery, zucchini, peas and mushrooms (or whatever vegetables you have on hand)

2 cups gravy

4-5 cups mashed potatoes

Seasoning to taste (salt and pepper, garlic powder, bouillon)

Egg wash (1 egg beat together with 1 T. water)

In a soup pot, put onions, carrots and celery and enough water to cover. Boil, covered, until carrots are fork-tender (about 10 minutes). Add remaining vegetables and continue cooking. Add gravy and heat to boiling. Thicken (or thin) as necessary to form a thick stew consistency. Add turkey and mix well, heat to boiling.

Pour into a casserole dish. Top with scoops of hot mashed potatoes. Brush with egg wash (to aid browning).

Put under broiler until potatoes are brown.

*(Use the same gravy base to fill a pot pie, or substitute biscuits for the mashed potatoes and bake in a 375-degree oven for 20 minutes or until biscuits are done)*

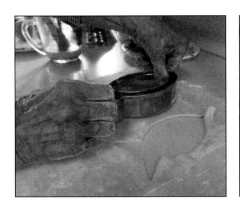
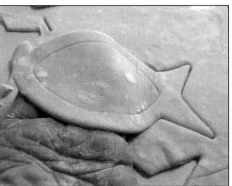

# Shrimp & Halibut Vol-au-vent

1 box puff pastry sheets
1 cup Alfredo sauce (homemade or prepared)
1 pound halibut roast, fillets or steaks
1 1/2 pounds jumbo shrimp
1 egg, whisked with 1 T. water (egg wash)
2 T. butter
Fresh parsley sprigs
Lemon wedges

Thaw puff pastry, separate sheets and roll out each on a floured board to size desired (large enough to cut out six forms. Brush first layer with egg wash and stack second layer on top.

Using a floured cutter, create shapes (We used a fish pattern). Place on parchment paper on baking sheet. Bake in a 400-degree oven for 20 to 25 minutes.

When cool, take a sharp knife and cut out lid shape. Remove lid, set aside. Scoop out excess dough to make room for filling.

Steam halibut, flake and remove any bones.

Prepare and/or heat white sauce. Stir in halibut.

Sauté de-veined and shelled shrimp in butter and garlic.

Fill shells with hot fish and sauce mixture. Hang shrimp on the sides and top with lid. Garnish with lemon wedges and fresh parsley.

(*Serves 6*)

# Sour Bratwurst from Frau Steinbauer

5 or 6 bratwurst
3 onions, sliced
2 T. oil
1 cup vinegar
Water (or beer)
1 t. caraway seeds

Fry sliced onions in oil over medium heat, stirring and cooking slow until onions are caramelized (about 20 minutes). Add vinegar and water (or beer) to cover onion, salt and pepper to taste. Bring to a boil. Add bratwurst. Cover and simmer for 30 minutes.

# Spanish-Style Quinoa

2 cups quinoa
4 cups water
1 T. garlic powder
1 T. oregano
2 T. cumin
1 15-ounce can chili
1 15-ounce can tomatoes

Rinse quinoa. Mix with other ingredients, bring to a boil, cover and simmer until liquid is absorbed and quinoa is tender. If necessary, add more liquid.

# Strata with Mushrooms and Broccoli
## (Breakfast Casserole)

This breakfast or brunch casserole is one that can be put together the night before and just popped into the oven in the morning. Optional add-on ingredients could include mushrooms, asparagus, peppers or zucchini.

8 slices French bread, chopped
1/2 cup chopped green onions
1 pound spicy pork sausage
1 1/2 cups broccoli crowns (parboiled)
2 cups shredded cheese
1/2 cup sliced olives (green or black)
2 T. fresh basil
9 eggs
2 1/2 cups milk
1 T. mustard
Pepper

Brown the sausage and green onions.

Put the bread cubes in a prepared 3-quart casserole. Top with half of the grated cheese. Next add browned sausage and onions, then the broccoli, olives and basil. Whisk the eggs and milk together with the mustard and pepper. Pour into the casserole. Top with remaining grated cheese.

Put in refrigerator overnight or all day until ready to bake.

Bake 1 hour in a 350-degree oven. Let sit 15 minutes before serving.

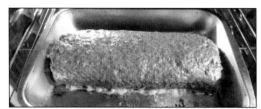

# Stuffed Meat Roll

### Stuffing

- 1 cube margarine
- 2 T. onion powder
- 2 t. celery seed
- 1/2 cup chopped basil
- 1 t. each salt and pepper
- 1 cup beef broth
- 5 cups cubed bread

Melt margarine in frying pan, add spices and beef broth. Pour over cubed bread and mix until bread is moist.

### Meat Roll

- 2 pounds hamburger (or any ground meat)
- 1 pound pork sausage
- 1 1/2 cups bread crumbs
- 2 eggs
- 1/2 cup ketchup
- 1 cup beef broth

Mix meats together, add crumbs, eggs, ketchup and broth. Mix well. Mound onto waxed paper and spread into a rectangle, about 1 1/2 inches thick.

Put stuffing down center of meat rectangle, leaving 1 inch clear at ends. Roll meat around stuffing (*Use waxed paper to help you roll it*). Pinch together ends and seam to seal.

Place roll seam-side down into greased 11x15-inch pan.

Bake uncovered at 360 degrees for one hour.

# Stuffed Sole

*This is simple, but good. I got this from Nellie and Eddie Vierra.*

- 8 sole fillets
- 8 slices soft bread, cubed
- 1 cup grated carrots
- 3/4 t. salt
- 1/2 t. pepper
- 1/4 cup melted butter
- Sour cream
- Parsley
- Lemon wedges

Make stuffing with soft bread crumbs, grated carrot, salt, pepper and melted butter. Add enough warm water to make it moist, but not sloppy.

Divide evenly between the fillets. Spread stuffing on each fillet, then roll up and place, seam side down, in buttered baking dish.

Bake 20 minutes at 375 degrees.

When it's done, spread with sour cream, garnish with parsley and lemon wedges.

# Sweet & Sour Meatloaf

*If you have any leftovers, this makes great sandwiches. And it freezes well. I usually make two at once and freeze one for later.*

- 2 pounds ground meat (1 pound beef and 1 pound pork sausage)
- 1 cup Italian-seasoned bread crumbs (If using plain crumbs, add basil, parsley and oregano)
- 1 t. salt
- 1 t. pepper
- 2 eggs
- 1 t. minced onion or onion powder
- 1 cup tomato sauce (or half of a 15-ounce can. Reserve the other half for glaze)
- Sweet and sour glaze (see below)

Mix meat, bread crumbs, spices, eggs and half the tomato sauce. Shape into a loaf (Pat it well to remove air pockets). Put in 9x12-inch pan (leave an inch between the meatloaf and the pan) and bake 50 minutes in a 350-degree oven. Pour prepared glaze over the meat and bake another 10 minutes.

# Sweet & Sour Glaze

- 2 T. brown sugar
- 2 T. cider vinegar
- 1/2 cup sugar
- 2 t. mustard
- 1 cup tomato sauce

Combine topping ingredients in a saucepan and bring to a boil. Simmer for 5 minutes. Use as directed.

# Taco-Flavored Chicken Wings

10 pounds chicken wings
4 packets taco seasoning

Put wings in shallow pan, single layer. Sprinkle with taco seasoning. Cover and refrigerate for several hours, turning over every 15 to 20 minutes. (For a smaller amount, use a Ziplock bag)

Bake in a 400-degree oven for 60 minutes, uncovered. Turn and stir halfway through.

---

# Turkey Sausage Patties

*Great for breakfast or dinner, or use mixture for meatloaf, meatballs or pizza topping.*

3 t. dried sage
1 t. brown sugar
1/4 t. crushed red pepper
flakes
1/4 t. nutmeg
1/4 t. pepper
3/4 t. salt
Pinch of allspice
1 pound ground turkey

Mix sugar and spices together, add to ground turkey and mix well.

Form into six balls and press into patties. Fry in oiled pan over medium heat until brown on both sides (15 to 20 minutes total).

You could also lightly brown and then put in a 350-degree oven for 15 minutes to finish cooking.

• *If making dinner patties, add 1/2 t. each of garlic powder, onion powder, green onions or chopped green or red pepper.*

• *If it looks like it won't hold*

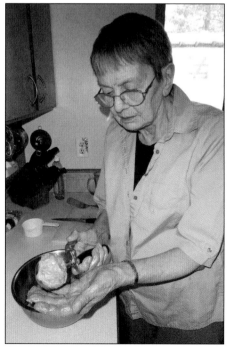

*together, add one egg and 1/2-cup bread crumbs.*

# Side Dishes

## Bread Dumplings

3/4 loaf of sliced bread, dried and cubed

5 slices bacon, chopped

1 small onion, minced

1/4 cup parsley

Salt and pepper to taste

4 eggs, beaten

1 1/2 cups milk

Flour (enough to make a solid mass)

Mix dried bread cubes and milk. Let stand a few minutes.

Sauté bacon and onion. Cool. Mix with parsley, seasoning and eggs. Add to bread and milk mixture. Work together with hands. Add flour as needed to make a solid mass. Make into balls (tennis ball size).

Place in boiling water. Boil, covered, for 20 minutes. Serve with gravy.

## Cabbage – German Style

Red cabbage, shredded

1 yellow onion, diced

1/4 cup butter

1 bay leaf

6 whole cloves

1/2 t. whole peppercorns

1 cup liquid (red wine, apple cider or mixture of broth and red wine vinegar. If using vinegar, add 1 T. sugar)

1/2 t. salt

Sauté onions in butter in Dutch oven until caramelized. Add cabbage, cook for 5 minutes. Add liquid and spices (tied in cheesecloth), bring to a boil. Cover and simmer on low (or place in 350-degree oven) for 2 hours, stirring occasionally. Add more liquid if needed.

If desired, thicken with flour before serving.

*Option: Add small diced apple to the onion and cabbage mixture.*

# Corn Fritters

1 1/2 cups sifted flour
2 1/2 t. baking powder
1 t. salt
1 egg, separated
1/2 cup milk
1 T. oil.
1 can whole kernel corn, drained.

Sift together flour, baking powder and salt. Beat egg white in a small bowl.

In a separate medium-sized bowl, mix milk, egg yolk and oil and corn. Stir in flour, blend well. Fold in egg white.

Drop by spoonful into hot oil, cook about 5 minutes, until golden brown.

*OPTION: For Clam and Corn Fritters, mix in an 8-ounce can drained minced clams to the milk and egg mixture.*

---

# Cucumbers in Sour Cream

Slice two cucumbers paper thin. Soak in salted water 30 minutes. Squeeze gently to drain, but don't mash.

Put in a bowl, sprinkle with salt and pepper to taste. Mix with sour cream to cover.

---

# Fried Vegetables

*Zucchini, egg plant, green tomatoes all work with this method. Add spices and seasoning to taste. Salt and pepper are the standards, but others will work, too. Oregano, basil, rosemary, thyme.*

Prepare three bowls. The first has seasoned flour. The second has a beaten egg or two (depending on how many you are fixing). The third has crumbs — cracker crumbs, bread crumbs or panko (whatever you have on hand).

Slice vegetables about 1/4-inch thick. Dip in flour, then egg, then crumbs.

Fry in oiled pan on medium heat.

Line oven-safe dish or pan with paper towel and put in warm oven. Put fried slices on pan in oven to drain and keep warm while finishing the rest of the batch.

Serve warm, with sour cream, blue cheese dressing or other sauce.

# Green Beans with Bacon & Onion

1 quart fresh or 2
   15-ounce cans of green
   beans (any variety)
4 slices bacon, cut into
   3/4-inch pieces
1 small onion, chopped
1 cup sliced mushroom
   (optional)

Put green beans (with juice or water enough to cover) in a saucepan. Add bacon, onion and mushroom. Bring to a boil and simmer for 30 minutes. Salt and pepper to taste.

# Marinated Tomatoes

2 large ripe tomatoes,
   sliced 1/3-inch thick
1/3 cup sugar
1 cup apple cider vinegar
1/2 t. each of salt and
   pepper
1 t. dried minced onion
1 t. minced fresh parsley
   (or dried parsley)

Mix sugar and vinegar together until sugar is dissolved. Add spices. Put in container with a tight lid (that can be turned upside down) and add tomato slices. Put in refrigerator for several hours, turning over every so often to spread the marinade around.

# Mashed yams

2 large yams
1/2 cube margarine or
   butter
Salt
2 t. onion powder
1/4 cup sweetener (sugar,
   brown sugar, agave)

Peel yams and cut into cubes. Put in pan, cover with water and bring to a boil. Cook until tender. Drain well. Add margarine, salt, onion powder and sweetener. Whip in mixer for 5 minutes.

# Mom's Spinach

*This works for any greens - kale, chard, spinach, beet greens.*

Spinach (fresh or frozen, chopped) *(A 10-ounce package of spinach will serve two people if they like spinach, or more if they just want a little bit)*

Cider vinegar

Olive oil

Salt and pepper

Hard boiled egg (chopped, but save some slices for garnish)

Cook spinach, drain well. Put in bowl, add salt, pepper, vinegar and oil to taste, mix well. Mix in chopped egg. Top with egg slices for garnish.

# Onion Fritters

2 cups cold mashed potatoes

1 egg

1/2 cup bread or cracker crumbs

1 large onion, chopped

Salt and pepper

Enough milk to make a thick batter

Mix all together. Drop by spoonfuls into hot oil. Flatten to form a patty and brown on both sides.

*These go well with sausage or bratwurst and a salad. Or they can be served as main dish with salad and fruit.*

The snowmobilers pose in front of the house in December 2016, the same house that's featured on the cover of this book. Pictured, from left, Adam Granzer, Stephan McDaniels, Tony Moran, Kimberly McDaniels and Shadee Berger.

# Orange Rice

2 cups rice

1 1/3 cup diced celery

6 T. butter

4 T. grated orange rind

1 1/2 cups orange juice (takes about three oranges, or use prepared juice)

4 cups water

2 t. soy sauce

2 t. celery seed

3 t. salt

1 T. onion powder

Into a 2-quart casserole (with a tight lid), mix in order given. Bake in a 350-degree oven for one hour. Goes well with chicken or pork. Serves 12 (freezes well).

*(I use long-grain white rice. You could use brown rice or quinoa, but might need to increase the total amount of liquid.)*

---

# Pate de Pommes de Terre (Potato Pie)

**Crust**

2 1/2 cups flour

1 1/4 t. salt

1 T. sugar

1/2 cup shortening

1/4 cup margarine

3 1/2 T. water (or so)

Mix dry ingredients well. Cut in shortening and margarine. Add water, mix until dough is smooth. Set aside, covered with waxed paper.

**Filling**

7 cups thinly sliced potatoes

2 t. salt

1/8 t. pepper

1 large onion, thinly sliced

2 t. margarine

1 T. milk

Sour cream

Mix together potatoes, onions, salt and pepper.

Divide pastry in two, with one ball slightly larger.

Roll out as for regular pie crust, the bottom about 1 inch larger than the top.

Place bottom crust in pie plate. Pile on potato and onion mixture. Top with margarine. Cover with top crust and brush with milk.

Crimp bottom and top crust edges together to seal. Slice a circle in the top center (for later removing the top to add sour cream).

Bake for 1 hour and 15 minutes in 350-degree oven.

**To serve:** Lift center circle, add sour cream, sprinkle with parsley and replace the top. Serve slightly warm or at room temperature.

# Potato Pancakes

*Some recipes call for adding flour, but this is the German way, according to my sources.*

3 medium-sized
   potatoes, grated
2 eggs
Salt and pepper
   to taste

Mix grated potatoes, eggs and seasonings together until well-coated.

Heat oil in a frying pan over medium heat. Put a heaping tablespoon of potato mixture in pan and flatting slightly.

Fry to golden brown and turn over. Put on paper towel-lined pan while cooking the remaining pancakes.

Serve with applesauce. Goes well with schnitzel.

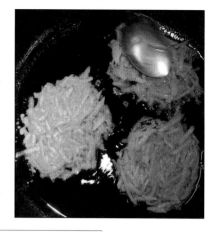

# Potato Planks

Large potatoes, sliced the
   long way, about 1/4-inch
   thick
Butter
Salt and pepper
Garlic powder
Thyme
Parmesan cheese

Heat oven to 350 degrees. Melt butter in baking pan. Put potato slices in pan, turning to coat both sides in butter. Mix seasonings and cheese together, sprinkle over potatoes. Bake for 30 minutes (or until tender).

## Another option:
# Yam & Potato Medallions

Slice yams and potatoes into medallions. Heat oil and seasoning of choice in frying pan. Cook medallions over medium heat, turning over once or twice.

*Or ... put them on a greased baking sheet in a 350-degree oven for 20 minutes, or until tender. Turn over at least once.*

# Rice & Cheese Cakes

2/3 cup cooked rice
2 eggs, beaten (reserve half for coating)
1 t. mustard
1 T. chopped parsley
3/4 cup grated cheese
1/4 cup flour
1/2 cup bread crumbs
Oil for frying

Mix together rice, one beaten egg, mustard, parsley and grated cheese and form cakes (3-inches in diameter and 3/4-inch thick).

Dip cakes into flour, then egg, then bread crumbs.

Fry in oil until brown on both sides.

# Stovetop Rice Pilaf

4-5 cups cooked rice
1/2 cup chopped peppers
1/2 cup chopped onions
1/2 cup margarine
1 t. garlic powder

Cook rice according to directions.

Sauté peppers and onions in butter. Add garlic. Mix with hot, cooked rice.

# Swiss Chard Bundles with Sausage

2 pounds large green Swiss chard leaves
1 pound spicy breakfast sausage
1 cup sliced mushrooms
2 large eggs
1/2 t. salt
1/2 t. pepper
4 green onions, chopped
2 cups grated cheese (cheddar or mozzarella)
1 1/2 T. oil
1/2 cup chicken broth

Wash and trim chard leaves, cutting stem even with leaf. Finely chop stems. Set aside.

Blanch chard leaves for 30 seconds in boiling water. Drain well.

Brown sausage, breaking up clumps. Add onions, chard stems and mushrooms and cook until tender.

Cool. Place in bowl. Add eggs and cheese, mix well.

Spread out individual chard leaves (if necessary, use two smaller leaves) to make a wrap that is 8x5 inches. Add 1/4 cup of sausage mixture to center. Fold sides into a bundle, place seam side down in greased baking dish. Drizzle with olive oil. Add broth to dish and cover. Bake in a 350-degree oven for 35 to 40 minutes (until egg is set).

# Tomato Dumplings

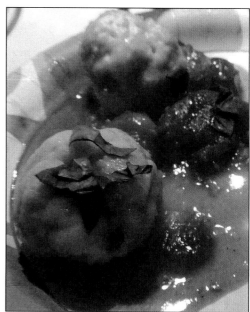

1/4 cup butter
1/4 cup chopped celery
1/2 cup chopped onion
1/2 cup chopped green
   pepper
1 bay leaf
1 quart canned tomatoes
   (or 2 28-ounce cans)
1 cup flour
1 1/2 t. baking powder
1/2 t. salt
2 T. butter, melted
1 egg
1/3 cup milk
2 T. chopped fresh basil
   or dill (Optional)

Melt 1/4 cup butter in saucepan and sauté celery, onion and green pepper — about 3 minutes. Add tomatoes (with juice) and bay leaf. Heat to boiling.

Blend dry ingredients. Beat egg and milk (add basil or dill if desired) and add to flour mixture, mixing only until moist. Divide into six spoonfuls and drop into boiling tomato mixture.

Boil gently for 20 minutes, covered. (Do not lift lid — the cardinal rule of all dumplings.)

Makes 6 dumplings.

## ALTERNATIVE

**Sauce:**

1 cup diced celery
1 T. salt
1 t. pepper
1 T. onion powder
1 T. sugar (or other
   sweetener such as
   agave)
1 cup chopped
   mushrooms
2 T. fresh basil
8 cups canned
   tomatoes (4 28-ounce
   cans)

Bring all but the basil to boil, cover and simmer for 15 minutes.

**Dumplings:**

2 cups flour
4 t. baking powder
1/2 t. salt
2 t. butter
3/4 cup milk

Mix and form into 2-inch balls. Drop on top of simmering tomatoes. Cover and cook for 20 minutes. (Do not lift lid.)

Before serving, sprinkle chopped basil on top.

# Twice-Baked Potato Boats

4 medium potatoes
8 T. butter
1 t. onion powder
Salt and pepper
Milk
4 T. grated dry cheese
(Parmesan or Romano,
but cheddar works, too)
Paprika and parsley

Bake potatoes. When done, cut in half length-wise (making eight boats). Scoop potato into a mixing bowl. Add butter (2 T. for each potato), onion powder, salt and pepper and enough milk to make a light, but not soupy, mixture. It should be the consistency of mashed potatoes.

Divide into the shells and sprinkle with cheese. If desired, sprinkle with paprika and parsley.

Bake on a cookie sheet to baking pan in a 400-degree oven until cheese is melted (about 15 minutes)

These freeze well. To use, put frozen potato boats on a baking sheet in a 375-degree oven for 20 minutes.

# Yorkshire Pudding

12 T. drippings from roast
6 eggs
3 cups milk
3 cups flour
2 1/4 t. salt

Put roasting pan with drippings in the oven to heat while mixing batter.

Combine batter ingredients, beat until smooth. Pour into hot pan.

Bake in 400-degree oven for 30 minutes.

Cut into squares and serve with roast and au jus.

# Zucchini Boats

1 large zucchini (12 inches long)
1 green pepper, diced
1 chopped tomato (drained)
1/2 cup dry bread crumbs
1/2 cup grated cheddar cheese
Salt and Pepper
2 T. butter

Cut zucchini in half, length-wise and then crosswise (to make four pieces).

Top each piece with green pepper and tomato. Dot with butter. Add salt and pepper to taste. Sprinkle with bread crumbs and cover with grated cheese.

Bake in a covered baking dish at 350 degrees for 20 minutes. Remove lid and bake 15 minutes longer.

# Zucchini Fritters

2 medium-sized zucchini, grated
1 t. salt
1 carrot, grated
2 T. minced onion
2 T. minced parsley
1 egg
1/2 cup flour
1/4 t. pepper

In a colander, mix zucchini and salt. Let drain 15 minutes, squeezing out excess liquid with back of a spoon.

Mix zucchini, carrot, onion, parsley, egg, flour and pepper.

Heat about 1/4-inch oil in skillet. For each fritter, place about 1/4 cup zucchini mixture into pan, flatten into a patty. Fry until first side is brown, turn, fry second side until brown. Drain on paper towels.

Winters in Plain come with some challenges, including snow, cold and power outages. Keeping a stocked pantry makes dinnertime easier, no matter the circumstances. A freak storm downed trees in December 2012, including this big one near the old chicken house. Another tree hit the power line to the house, leaving us without power through Christmas. This photo was taken by Chauncy Burgess, who was staying with us at the time.

# Desserts

## Amish Oatmeal Pie

1 9-inch unbaked pie crust

**Beat together:**
- 3 T. flour
- 1 cup sugar
- 4 eggs

**Add:**
- 2 T. melted butter
- 1 t. vanilla
- 1 T. grated orange peel
- 1 cup corn syrup
- 1 cup instant oatmeal (plain)
- Pinch of salt
- 1/2 t. cinnamon

Mix, pour into pie shell and bake in 350-degree oven for 45 to 50 minutes.

## Apple Kuchen

- 1 cup butter or margarine (at room temperature)
- 1 cup sugar
- 2 eggs
- 3 cups flour, sifted
- 3 t. baking powder
- 1 t. rum extract or vanilla
- Sliced apples or plums
- Cinnamon and sugar

Grease and flour a 10-inch round cake pan (or something similar with 2-inch sides, such as a spring-form pan.)

Mix butter and sugar until creamy. Add eggs and rum (or vanilla), mix until smooth. Add flour and baking powder. Dough will be thick. With floured knuckles, press evenly into prepared pan.

Arrange fruit slices on top (leave some space between slices), pressing gently into dough.

Bake at 360 degrees for 40 minutes (or until toothpick comes out clean). Remove from oven and, while still warm, sprinkle with a mixture of sugar and cinnamon. Don't put the sugar on the fruit before baking or it will make the juice ooze out of the fruit.

*Over the River ...*

# Applesauce Cake

*(No eggs and no milk!)*

1/2 cup oil
1 cup brown sugar
2 cups applesauce
4 1/2 cups flour
1 t. soda
1 t. salt
2 t. baking powder
1 T. vanilla or rum extract

Mix well. Pour into a greased and floured 9x13-inch pan. Bake 1 hour in preheated 325-degree oven.

**Option:** Add 1/2 cup raisins covered in flour.

# Baked Custard

2 cups milk
1/2 cup sugar
1/8 t. salt
2 eggs
1/2 t. vanilla
Nutmeg
Caramel sauce

Preheat oven to 300 degrees.

Mix together milk, sugar and salt. Add eggs and vanilla, beat well.

Pour into custard cups or ramekins (or baking dish). Sprinkle top with nutmeg.

Place cups in baking pan. Fill larger pan with hot water to within 1/2 inch of the custard-filled containers. Bake until set. It takes about 40 minutes. Check by sticking a knife in the center. If it comes out clean it's done. Cool. Top with caramel sauce to serve.

# Baker's Cream

*This frosting is made with granulated sugar and has the texture of whipped cream. It can be used for frosting cakes or as filling for cakes or even cream puffs.*

**In a small saucepan blend:**
- 5 tablespoons flour
- 1 cup milk

Blend well and cook to a thick paste, stirring constantly. Let stand until cool.

**In a mixing bowl, put:**
- 1 cup butter or margarine (at room temperature)
- 1 cup granulated sugar
- 1 t. vanilla

Beat butter, sugar and vanilla until light and fluffy. Gradually add cooled paste, mixing after each addition. Beat on high speed for 10 minutes, until it looks like whipped cream.

It can be kept in refrigerator, covered tightly.

# Banana Cream Cake

- 1 sheet cake (white, vanilla or chocolate)
- Banana cream pie filling
- Banana slices

Bake the cake in a 9x13-inch pan (use a mix or bake a 1-egg cake from scratch). Cool.

Spread prepared pudding on top, then banana slices, then more pudding.

Top with whipped cream or meringue.

# Basic Custard

- 2 cups milk
- 5 eggs, whipped
- 2/3 cup sugar
- 1/2 t. salt
- 2 t. vanilla or rum extract
- 4 T. cornstarch
- 1/2 cup cold water

Whisk together milk, eggs, sugar and salt. Heat in saucepan on medium until hot, but not boiling. Remove from heat.

Dissolve cornstarch in 1/2 cup cold water. Mix with about a cup of the hot egg mixture and whisk it into the remaining egg mixture. Return to heat, stirring constantly until it thickens, about 5 minutes or so. (The mixture will cling to the spoon). Be careful not to overcook or the eggs will curdle. Stir in vanilla or other flavoring.

Pour into serving dishes. (To avoid developing a skin on top, cover with plastic wrap.)

# Carrot Pineapple Cake

2 cups flour
2 t. baking powder
1 1/2 t. soda
2 T. cinnamon
1 T. salt
2 cups sugar
1 1/2 cups oil
4 eggs
2 cups grated carrots
1 small can crushed
  pineapple with juice
1/2 cup nuts

Mix oil, eggs, carrots and pineapple. Add dry ingredients, mix well. Fold in nuts. Pour into greased and floured cake pans (Makes three 8-inch or 9-inch rounds).

Bake in a 350-degree oven for 40 minutes.

Cool.

Ice with cream cheese frosting or plain vanilla frosting. Or simply sprinkle top with powdered sugar.

# Cheesecake

### Filling

- 2 eggs
- 2 8-ounce packages of cream cheese at room temperature
- 1/2 cup sugar
- 1 T. lemon juice or vanilla
- 1/2 t. salt

### Topping

- 1 1/2 cups sour cream
- 2 T. sugar
- 1/2 t. vanilla
- 1/8 t. salt

### Graham cracker crust

- 1 1/2 cups graham cracker crumbs
- 6 T. melted butter

Preheat oven to 375 degrees.

Mix graham cracker crumbs and melted butter, press into the bottom of a 9-inch springform pan. Bake for 7 minutes at 375 degrees.

Mix filling ingredients and pour on top of crust. Bake in 375 degree oven for 20 minutes. Remove from oven and let cool. Heat oven to 450 degrees. Mix sour cream topping and pour over cooled cake.

Bake for 5 minutes, cool, chill in refrigerator.

# Chocolate Cake

*No eggs and no milk!*

3 cups flour
2 cups sugar
6 T. cocoa
1 t. salt
2 t. soda
1/2 cup oil
2 t. vanilla
2 T. vinegar
2 cups cold water

Sift dry ingredients together into large mixing bowl.

Add oil, vanilla, vinegar and water.

Stir well and put in a greased and floured 9x13-inch pan. Bake in 350-degree oven for 25 minutes. Cool. Frost. Serve out of the pan.

Also works for cupcakes or smaller cake pans. And it freezes well.

# Chocolate No-Bake Cookies

*I don't usually like chocolate and peanut butter, but I like these.*
*And they do freeze well.*

2 cups sugar
4 t. cocoa
1/4 cup butter
1/2 cup milk
3 cups oatmeal
1/2 cup peanut butter
1 t. vanilla
1/2 cup nuts or coconut

Heat sugar, cocoa, butter and milk in sauce pan, boil for 1 minute.

Mix oatmeal, peanut butter, vanilla and nuts together. Pour boiled mixture over the top and mix well. Drop by spoonfuls onto waxed paper. Let cool.

# No-Bakes with a Twist

*No peanut butter, extra seeds*

1 c. brown sugar
1/4 cup butter
2 t. cocoa
1/4 cup milk

Mix in large saucepan, bring to a boil and boil 2 minutes, stirring once or twice.

**Mix together:**
1 cup oatmeal
1/2 cup coconut
1/4 cup sesame seeds
1/2 cup sunflower seeds
(or chopped peanuts)

Remove sugar mixture from heat, add 1/2 t. vanilla and oat/seed mixture. Drop by spoonful onto waxed paper. Cool.

# Chocolate Pudding Cake

*Granddaughter Daysha has requested this dessert from time-to-time during her visits, which we always enjoy.*

1 cup flour
2 t. baking powder
1 t. salt
2/3 cup sugar
6 T. cocoa
1/2 cup milk
1 t. vanilla
2 T. melted margarine
1/2 cup chopped nuts
  (optional)
1 cup brown sugar
1 1/2 cups boiling water

Sift flour, baking powder, salt, sugar and 2 tablespoons of the cocoa together three times.

Combine milk and margarine, add to dry ingredients, beat until smooth.

Stir in nuts. spread in a 6-cup casserole dish.

Mix brown sugar with the remaining 4 tablespoons of cocoa. Sprinkle over batter. Pour the boiling water over the top.

Bake 350 degrees for 50 minutes.

The cake will come to the top and the pudding will form on the bottom while it bakes.

*Over the River ...*

# Chocolate Zucchini Cake

1 2/3 cup sugar
1/2 cup butter (softened)
2 eggs
1/2 cup oil
1 1/2 t. vanilla
2 1/2 cups flour
1/3 cup cocoa
1 t. baking soda
1/2 t. salt
1/2 cup buttermilk
2 cups shredded zucchini
3/4 cup chopped pecans
1 cup chocolate chips

Preheat oven to 325 degrees. Grease and flour 13x9-inch pan. Beat sugar, butter and oil until well blended. Add eggs, one at a time, beating well after each.

Add vanilla.

Sift together flour, cocoa, soda and salt. Add to sugar mixture alternately with buttermilk, beating well. Stir in zucchini. Top with nuts and chocolate chips.

Beat for 55 minutes or until toothpick comes clean.

# Coffee Cake

2 cups sugar
1 T. cinnamon
1 cup shortening
4 eggs, separated
1/4 t. salt
3 cups flour
3 t. baking powder
1 cup milk
1 t. vanilla or almond
  extract

Make a mixture of 1/2 cup sugar and cinnamon.

Mix well and set aside. Cream shortening, gradually add 1 1/2 cups sugar and cream well. Add egg yolks one at a time and beat.

Combine flour and baking powder. Add to creamed mixture alternately with milk. Combine salt and egg whites and beat until stiff. Add flavoring and mix well. Then fold the two mixtures together. Spoon layers of batter into a well-oiled bundt pan, with cinnamon mixture on top of each layer of batter. Try to use all the cinnamon mixture.

Bake one hour in a 375-degree oven. Let cool 10 minutes. Loosen sides with a knife and turn out on rack to cool completely. Sift powdered sugar over top and sides of cake.

# Cookies (Favorites from the Plain Bakery)

*These three cookie recipes from the Plain Bakery were the best sellers.*
*All of these recipes can be divided to make smaller batches. All of these cookies freeze well.*

## Oatmeal Cookies

1 1/2 cups shortening
2 cups brown sugar
1 cup white sugar
2 eggs
2 t. vanilla
2 t. salt
1/2 cup water
2 cups flour
1 t. soda
6 cups oatmeal

Mix together everything but oatmeal, mixing well. Stir in oatmeal. You may have to get in and mix with your hands.

Drop by tablespoonful onto a greased cookie sheet. Wet your hands and press dough evenly until thin.

Bake in a 350-degree oven for 15 minutes. Don't over bake or cookies will be crisp, rather than chewy.

Store in an air-tight container.

## Molasses Cookies

2 1/4 cups shortening
3 cups brown sugar
3 eggs
2/3 cup molasses
3/4 t. salt
6 t. soda
1 1/2 t. clovers
3 t. cinnamon
3 t. ginger
6 1/2 cups flour

Mix first five ingredients. Sift together dry ingredients. Mix all together. This is a good time to toss away the spoon and use your hands. Dough will be very thick. Form dough into balls about the size of large walnuts. Place on cookie sheets, about 4 inches apart. With glass dipped in sugar, press thin or use the wet hand method (as described in the Oatmeal Cookie recipe).

Bake in a 350-degree oven for 12 to 15 minutes. Don't over bake.

## Peanut Butter Cookies

2 cups shortening
1 1/2 cups peanut butter
4 cups white or brown sugar
4 eggs
1 cup milk
4 t. vanilla
5 cups flour
4 t. baking powder
1 t. salt

Mix together first six ingredients in order given, mixing well. Sift together the dry ingredients and add. Mix well. Drop by spoonfuls onto greased baking sheet and flatten with a fork dipped in sugar. Bake at 350 degrees for 15 minutes.

# Cream Cheese Pie

3 8-ounce packages of cream cheese
1 cup sugar
4 eggs
1 1/2 tsp. lemon juice

**Topping:**
Mix together:
1 cup sour cream
1/3 cup sugar

Whip together cream cheese, 1 cup sugar, eggs and lemon extract.

Pour into baked pie crust (regular, oatmeal or graham cracker). Bake for 50 minutes in 325-degree oven.

Add sour cream topping (spread over pie). Bake at 375 degrees for 10 minutes more. Cool and refrigerate.

Before serving, decorate with fruit: kiwi slices, strawberries, cherries.

(**Hint**: *Use wet knife to slice*)

# Dried Fruit Bars

*I found this recipe in a professional baker trade publication years ago.*

7 eggs
2 pounds brown sugar
1/4 cup vanilla
4 1/3 cups flour
13 ounces dried fruit
  (prunes, apricots,
  cherries, cranberries)
14 ounces chopped nuts
Orange zest (optional, but
  goes well with prunes)

Steam fruit for 10 minutes.

Put eggs in large sauce pan and heat with sugar to mix. Heat on low to dissolve the sugar, but not warm enough to cook the eggs. Add vanilla, then flour. Mix until combined. Add the fruit (which has been steamed for 10 minutes and then cooled).

Mix by hand or beat on low. Pour onto large cookie sheet lined with waxed paper or parchment and spread evenly.

Bake 20 minutes in a 350-degree oven.

Take out of the oven and flip onto another cookie sheet, remove parchment paper to prevent it sticking. Flip back over onto cooling rack so right side is up. Cool. Cut into bars. Store in air-tight container or freeze.

Makes 70 bars.

# Eclairs

1 cup flour
1/4 t. salt
1 cube margarine
1 cup water
4 whole eggs

Put water, salt and margarine in a large sauce pan and bring to a boil. Add flour all at once, stirring continually until a ball is formed and the dough leaves the sides of the pan.

Remove from heat and cool slightly. Add eggs, one at a time, beating after each addition. Mixture should be a creamy, solid mass.

Shape the dough into long narrow strips, 1.5 inches wide by 5 inches long. Place on greased cookie sheet, leaving 2 inches between each piece. Bake in 450-degree oven for 10 minutes, turn oven to 400 and bake for 25 minutes more.

Remove from oven and cool.

Once cool, slit the length of one side and fill with rich custard. Frost with chocolate glaze or frosting.

**Alternate:** Use the same dough for full-size cream puffs, or for small puffs that can be used for crab or tuna puffs, popular appetizers at our family gatherings.

# Frozen Peanut Butter Pie

Oatmeal pie crust
8-ounce package of
  cream cheese
1 cup creamy peanut
  butter
3/4 cup sugar
1 t. vanilla
2 cups Cool Whip
  topping, divided

Prepare oatmeal pie crust in 9-inch pie plate.

Beat cream cheese, peanut butter, sugar and vanilla until well blended. Stir in 1 1/2 cups whipped topping. Spoon onto crust. Freeze 4 hours or until firm.

Remove from freezer for 30 minutes before slicing and serving. Top with remaining Cool Whip.

# Ice Cream Pie

1 baked pie shell
8 ounces cream cheese
  (at room temperature)
1/3 cup sugar
1 t. vanilla or rum flavoring
1 cup whipping cream
  (unwhipped)
1 T. sugar
1 quart ice cream (black
  cherry is a popular pick,
  but others will do as well)

Mix together cream cheese and flavoring. Whip cream and sugar and fold together with cream cheese mixture. Pour into pie shell and freeze (at least 2 hours).

Soften quart of ice cream and spread over the top.

Freeze (at least an hour), but it can be made ahead of time.

Take out of the freezer 15 minutes before serving.

# Jelly Roll

4 eggs
3/4 cup sugar
1 t. vanilla
1 cup sifted flour
1 t. baking powder
Prepared filling or jelly

Put eggs in a mixing bowl (medium size with narrow bottom). Put bowl over pan of hot water. Beat the eggs until fluffy and light in color. Start adding sugar gradually, beating constantly. The process takes about 5 minutes. (The hot water helps dissolve the sugar more quickly).

Add vanilla.

Sift together dry ingredients. Fold into the egg mixture.

Grease and line a jelly roll pan with waxed paper that has been greased. Dump dough onto pan and spread evenly.

Bake at 400 degrees for 12 minutes. Do not over bake.

While still hot, turn cake onto a damp dish towel. Peel off paper quickly and roll up in towel. With seam side down, cover with plastic wrap and put in refrigerator.

When cool, unroll gently and spread with filling or whipped cream and re-roll. Sift powdered sugar on top or, as an alternative, roll in 1 cup of unsweetened coconut that has been chopped fine in a blender or food processor. (The coconut will stick better if roll is brushed lightly with jelly.)

For a chocolate roll, add 3 T. cocoa to dry ingredients. Fill with whipped cream or Cool Whip.

Cover filled roll with plastic, leave in refrigerator for a day before slicing. The roll also will freeze well.

# Lemon Pie Cake

1 unbaked pie crust
1 1/2 cups sugar
2 T. melted margarine
1/3 cup flour
1/4 t. salt
1/2 t. grated lemon rind
5 T. lemon juice
3 eggs, separated
1 1/4 cups milk

Blend sugar, margarine, flour, salt, lemon peel and juice. Beat egg yolks, combine with milk and add to lemon mixture. Beat egg whites until stiff, gently fold into other mixture.

Pour into unbaked crust.

Bake in 375-degree oven for 50 minutes. Cool. Top with powdered sugar or whipped cream.

# Lemon Pie Filling with Meringue

1 cup sugar

1 1/4 cups water

1 T. margarine

1/4 cup cornstarch

3 T. cold water

6 T. lemon juice

1 t. grated lemon rind

3 egg yolks

2 T. milk

1 egg white, stiffly beaten

1 9-inch baked pie shell
   (or tart-sized baked
   shells)

Combine sugar, water and butter. Cook until sugar dissolves. Add cornstarch (dissolved in cold water). Cook slowly until clear, about 8 minutes. Add lemon juice and rind. Cook 2 minutes.

Slowly add the egg yolks that have been beaten with 2 tablespoons of milk. Bring to a boil.

Remove from heat and let cool. Once cool, fold in stiffly beaten egg white.

Pour into baked shell and top with meringue.

### Meringue:
2 egg whites

2 T. sugar

1/2 t. cream of tartar

Beat egg whites until foamy. Continue beating while adding cream of tartar. Add sugar, 1 tablespoon at a time until it holds its shape. Spread over pie (clear to edges). Bake 350 degrees for 10-15 minutes (until brown).

# Lemon Squares

1 cup flour
1/2 cup margarine
1/4 cup powdered sugar

Blend together and press in the bottom of an 8x8-inch square pan. Bake for 20 minutes in a 350-degree oven.

While the crust bakes, beat together the following:

2 eggs
2 T. lemon juice
1/2 T. lemon zest
1 cup sugar
1/2 t. baking powder
1/4 t. salt

Pour over crust. Sprinkle lemon zest on top and bake for another 20 minutes.

It will puff up and then flatten as it bakes. Remove from oven. When cool, sprinkle with powdered sugar.

These freeze well.
*Alternative* ... *Orange Squares: Substitute concentrated orange juice and orange zest for lemon.*

# Meringues

4 egg whites
1/2 t. salt
1 t. cream of tartar
1 cup sugar

Beat egg whites until foamy. Add salt and cream of tartar. Add sugar, 1 tablespoon at a time, beating after each addition. When all has been added, continue to beat until peaks form.

Put a sheet of parchment paper on a cookie sheet. Shape whipped mixture into 12 individual shells (or make one large shell).

With the back of a wet spoon (it won't stick if it's wet), hollow out the center. Bake at 250 degrees for an hour.

Cool. Store in air-tight container.

Fill with fruit and whipped cream, or ice cream.

# Meringues II

*This recipe uses vinegar and baking powder rather than cream of tartar …*

8 egg whites
1/4 t. salt
1 t. baking powder
2 cups sugar
2 t. vanilla
2 t. vinegar

Beat eggs until frothy, add baking powder and salt. Beat until stiff. Add sugar, 1 T. at a time, beating constantly at high speed until stiff and glossy. Add vinegar and vanilla slowly, continuing to beat. Cover baking sheet with parchment paper (or waxed paper) and outline a form into an oval, about 2 inches thick, with shallow dip in the center.

Bake in 275-degree oven until dry (It will not brown). Shut oven off and leave door closed until cool.

Fill and serve.

**See the Sponge Layer Cake recipe on page 132 to use the egg yolks.**

# Nantucket Pudding

*This is a quick and easy dessert when you're in a pinch.*

1 quart berries
3/4 cup water
3/4 cup sugar (or to taste)
1/2 t. salt
2 heaping T. cornstarch

Bring berries and water to a boil, simmer for 10 minutes.

Add sugar (or other sweetener), to taste, and salt. Stir to dissolve. Remove from heat.

Dissolve cornstarch in water. Add to fruit mixture, return to heat, stir and cook until thick. (It's thick when it hangs off the spoon.)

Put in serving dishes. Cool to lukewarm. Cover with plastic, put in refrigerator. Top with whipped cream and berry garnish when time to serve.

# Oatmeal Fruit Bars

3 cups flour
2 t. soda
1/2 t. salt
2 cups brown sugar
3 1/2 cups oatmeal
1 1/2 cups margarine
1 cup (or more)
   mincemeat or thick jam

Mix first 5 ingredients together in a large bowl. Cut in margarine and mix until crumbly.

Press half of the mixture into the bottom of a 9x13-inch pan. Spread evenly with mincemeat or jam, going clear to edge. Sprinkle the remaining crumbs over the top. Press down gently.

Bake at 350 degrees for 30 minutes. Cool. Cut into squares. Store in air-tight container. Freezes well.

# Orange Pound Cake

3 1/4 cups sifted flour
1/4 t. salt
1/4 t. baking soda
1 cup, plus 2 T. butter, softened
8 ounces cream cheese, softened
3 cups sugar
6 eggs
1 t. vanilla
1/4 cup orange juice

**Glaze:**
1/2 cup orange juice
1/2 cup sugar

Preheat oven to 325 degrees. Butter and flour a bundt-type pan.

Sift together flour, salt and soda. Set aside.

Mix butter and cream cheese in mixer, beat until light and fluffy (about 5 minutes). Turn mixer to low and slowly add sugar. Add eggs, one at a time, scraping bowl after each egg. Mix in vanilla.

Add dry ingredients, alternately with orange juice, to egg mixture, mixing just until blended.

Spread batter into pan. Bake 1 hour and 15 minutes (until toothpick inserted comes out clean). Cool on a rack for 15 minutes.

Make glaze by stirring together orange juice and sugar in a small saucepan. Heat mixture, stirring constantly, until sugar is dissolved.

Turn cake out onto a cooling rack. Brush with orange glaze and cool completely.

Serves 10.

# Peanut Butter Kisses

*(No cooking required)*

1/3 cup corn syrup
1/3 cup peanut butter
1/3 cup nonfat dry milk
1/3 cup powdered sugar
Chopped nuts (optional)

Combine corn syrup with peanut butter in a small bowl, mixing well. Gradually add nonfat dry milk and sifted powdered sugar.

Shape into 3/4-inch roll. If desired, roll in chopped nuts. Wrap in waxed paper and chill.

Cut into 24 1-inch pieces.

# Peanut Butter Pie

Baked pie shell
3 cups milk
1 cup sugar (brown or white)
3 eggs, well beaten
1/2 t. salt
1/4 cup corn starch
1/2 cup peanut butter (creamy or crunchy)
1 1/2 t. vanilla

In a large saucepan, heat milk, sugar, cornstarch and salt over medium heat, stirring constantly until thick and bubbly. Reduce heat. Cook and stir 2 minutes. Remove from heat.

Mix a small amount of the hot filling into beaten eggs then pour egg mixture back into the milk mixture. Return to heat and bring to a boil, stirring constantly for an additional 2 minutes.

Remove from heat. Mix in peanut butter and vanilla.

Allow it to cool until warm, then pour into baked and cooled pie crust.

If topping with meringue, do that now. Otherwise, chill, top with whipped cream before serving.

# Pie Crust

### Graham Cracker Crust

1 1/2 cups graham cracker crumbs
6 T. melted butter

Mix well, press into pie tin (9 to 11 inches) and bake for 7 minutes at 375 degrees.
Cool and fill.

### Oatmeal Pie Crust

1 1/2 cups oatmeal
3 T. butter or margarine
2 T. sugar

Grind oatmeal in a food processor or blender to desired consistency. Add butter and sugar and pulse until mixed.

Press into pie tin. Bake 10 minutes in 375-degree oven. Cool. Fill to suit.

### Mom's Fool-Proof Pie Crust
*(Makes five pie crusts)*

4 cups flour
1 T. salt
1 3/4 cup shortening or lard
1/2 cup cold water
1 T. vinegar
1 large egg
1 T. sugar

Stir together flour, salt and sugar. Cut in shortening. Beat eggs, water, vinegar. Mix all together with a fork. Divide into five balls and wrap in plastic.

Use immediately or refrigerate (up to five days. It can also be frozen. Recipe can be doubled.

# Pumpkin Pie

1 unbaked pie crust
2 eggs, slightly beaten
1 small (15-ounce) can pumpkin
3/4 cup sugar, plus 1 T. flour
1/2 t. salt
1 t. cinnamon
1/2 t. ginger
1/4 t. cloves
1 2/3 cups canned milk or light cream

Whisk all ingredients together and pour into unbaked pie shell. Bake at 425 degrees for 15 minutes, then reduce heat to 350 degrees and bake for another 45 minutes. Cool on wire rack. Chill. Top with whipped cream.

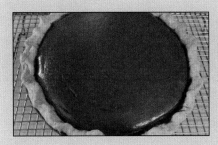

**Alternative:** Instead of canned pumpkin, use baked pumpking or winter squash that's been pureed. Add a little extra flour and use brown sugar instead of white sugar.

# Pumpkin Pudding

*This recipe started as Pumpkin Pie Walnut Squares, with a second layer of chopped nuts, brown sugar and margarine on top. But we found the extra sugar unnecessary, though it certainly can be added.*

**Crust:**
1 cup flour
1/2 cup oatmeal
1/2 cup brown sugar
1/2 cup margarine

**Filling:**
1 15-ounce can pumpkin
2 eggs
1 large can canned milk
3/4 cup sugar
1 t. cinnamon
3/4 t. pumpkin pie spice
1/2 t. salt

Mix and rub crust ingredients together until crumbly. Press into a 9x13-inch pan. Bake at 350 degrees for 15 minutes.

Combine filling ingredients, mix well and pour over baked crust. Return to oven and bake for 40 minutes (or until filling is set)

If you want the nut topping, mix 1/4 cup chopped walnuts, 2 T. margarine, 1/2 cup brown sugar until crumbly. Add to filling top after it has baked 20 minutes. Continue baking another 20 minutes until set.

# Rhubarb Custard Pie

1 pie crust

3 eggs

1 t. vanilla

1 cup sugar

Pinch of salt

4 cups rhubarb (cut in 1-inch pieces)

**Streusel topping**

Crumb together the following:

1 cup brown sugar

1 cup flour

1 cube margarine (1/4 pound)

1 t. cinnamon

Pinch of salt

Roll out pie crust, flute edges.

Fill crust almost to top of pie tin with sliced rhubarb. Beat together eggs, vanilla, sugar and salt. Pour over rhubarb.

Top with streusel mixture.

Bake at 400 degrees for 15 minutes. Reduce heat to 350 degrees and bake 40 minutes (or until done — toothpick test)

# Rhubarb Pudding Cake

2 cups sliced rhubarb

3 T. butter or margarine

1 1/2 cups sugar

1/2 cup bran flakes

3/4 cup sifted flour

1 t. baking powder

1/2 t. salt

1/2 cup milk

3 1/2 t. cornstarch

1/2 cup boiling water

Slice washed rhubarb into 1-inch lengths. Put into greased 8-inch-square baking dish. Cream together butter and 3/4 cup sugar. Stir in bran flakes until well blended.

Sift flour, measure, sift again with baking powder and 1/4 t. salt. Stir into creamed mixture alternately with milk. Spread batter evenly over rhubarb. Stir remaining 3/4 cup sugar, 1/4 teaspoon salt and cornstarch until blended. Sprinkle over batter. Pour boiling water over the top.

This dessert has a crisp topping over a moist cake and a sweet rhubarb pudding base.

# Rum Cake

*This cake is potent. It's better the second day (if it lasts that long).*

1 cup chopped pecans or walnuts
1 package yellow cake mix
1 package instant vanilla pudding
4 eggs
1/2 cup cold water
1/2 cup dark rum
1/3 cup oil
Glaze (see below)

Preheat oven to 325 degrees. Grease and flour a 10-inch tube pan. Sprinkle the nuts on the bottom of the pan. Mix cake mix, pudding, eggs, water, rum and oil. Beat well. Pour into pan and bake for 1 hour.

Cool to warm and invert on a cake plate. With a fork, prick top of cake (to make it easier to absorb the glaze).

Using a tablespoon, drizzle glaze over top and sides of cake (a pastry brush works, as well). Use all of the glaze.

### Glaze

1 cube margarine
1/3 cup water
1/2 cup sugar
1/2 cup dark rum

Melt margarine in sauce pan. Stir in water and sugar. Boil 5 minutes, stirring constantly. Remove from heat and stir in rum.

# Sour Cream Blueberry Cookies

1 cup margarine
1 cup sugar
1/2 cup sour cream (or buttermilk)
2 eggs
1 t. soda
3 cups flour
1 t. vanilla
3/4 cup blueberries (or nuts or raisins)

Cream together sugar and margarine. Sift together flour and soda. Mix all together. Fold in blueberries (Dust blueberries in flour before mixing).

Drop by spoonfuls onto greased cookie sheet.

Bake at 350 degrees for 10 minutes. Cookies will be pale.

# Sponge Layer Cake

*(Use up the egg yolks from making meringues on page 125)*

2 3/4 cups flour (measure after sifting)
1 T. baking powder
1 1/4 t. salt
2/3 cup butter, softened
2 cups sugar
7 egg yolks
1 1/4 cups milk
2 t. vanilla
Frosting of choice

Preheat oven to 350 degrees. Grease and flour three 9-inch round layer cake pans.

Sift together flour, baking powder and salt. Set aside.

In a bowl, beat egg yolks until thick and lemon colored. Set aside.

In a mixer bowl, beat butter and sugar until light and fluffy, scraping bowl occasionally. Beat in egg yolks. On low speed, alternately add dry ingredients and milk and vanilla, starting and ending with dry ingredients.

Divide into prepared pans (make sure batter is evenly spread).

Bake for 20 to 25 minutes (until golden). Turn out onto wire racks after cooling for 10 minutes.

Cool completely before frosting.

# Toffee Bars

1 cup margarine
1 cup brown sugar
1 cup chopped nuts
1/2 cup wheat germ
  (optional)
Whole graham crackers

Line a 9x13-inch pan with whole graham crackers (trying not to leave any space between).

Put butter and sugar in saucepan, boil for 3 minutes. Stir in nuts and wheat germ. Spread mixture over crackers. Bake for 10 minutes in 325-degree oven.

Cut into bars when almost cool.

# Walnut Spice Cake

*For those looking for options to cut carbs, this recipe is relatively low to start with and can be even lower is you use coconut flour and agave. Use spices or leave plain. Use vanilla or other flavorings or leave plain, perhaps depending on what kind of filling you intend to use.*

*We have been making a cream cheese and agave filling, with vanilla or lemon, along with sliced fruit — strawberries, blueberries, peaches, kiwi. Your imagination is the only limit.*

2 T. white flour
(or 1 T. coconut flour)
2 1/2 t. baking powder
4 eggs
1/2 cup sugar (or 1/3 cup
  agave)
1 cup walnuts or
  hazelnuts
1 t. cinnamon, ginger,
  cloves
1/2 t. vanilla

Sift together flour, baking powder and dry spices.

Place eggs, sugar and vanilla in a blender. Blend until smooth. Add nuts gradually and continue to blend until nuts are finely ground. Add sifted dry ingredients and mix well. Pour into two round cake pans with greased wax paper on the bottom. Bake in 350-degree oven for 20 minutes.

**Filling and Frosting**
  8 ounces cream
    cheese, softened
  Sweetener to taste
  Flavorings to taste

Whip together until smooth. Spread half cream cheese mixture on top of what will be the lower layer and on the bottom of what will be the top layer.

Place sliced fruit between layers. Spread remaining cream cheese mixture on top, decorate. Chill until ready to serve.

# Whoopie Pies

1 cube butter
1/2 cup lard or shortening
2 cups sugar
2 eggs
2 t. vanilla
4 cups flour
1 cup cocoa powder
3 t. cream of tartar
1 t. soda
1 t. salt
1 1/3 cup sour cream

**Filling for whoopie pie**
  1 1/2 cup
     marshmallow cream
  1 1/4 cup shortening
  1 cup powdered sugar
  1 T. vanilla
Cream all together.

Cream butter, lard and sugar. Add eggs and vanilla, then dry ingredients and sour cream, beating slow.

Make rounds (tennis ball size or smaller if you prefer) and place on a greased cookie sheet, leaving space between so they don't touch. Bake for 11 minutes in a 375-degree oven. Cool.

Put 1/2-inch filling (frosting) between two rounds to make sandwiches. Chill and wrap separately to freeze.

# Yellow Cucumber Cake

*If you are looking for something to do with those over-ripe cucumbers ...*

3 eggs
1 cup (less 2 tablespoons oil)
1 2/3 cup sugar
2 t. vanilla

2 cups peeled, seeded and grated yellow over-ripe cucumbers
3 cups flour
1/2 t. salt

1 T. cinnamon
3/4 t. nutmeg
1 t. baking soda
1/4 t. baking powder

Beat eggs until light. Add oil, sugar, cucumbers and vanilla. Blend in sifted dry ingredients. Pour into a greased and floured 9x13-inch pan (or two loaf pans). Bake at 350 degrees for 25 to 30 minutes.

Chopped nuts can be added. Frost if desired, but it's good plain.

# Extras

## Cranberry Relish

*Great with Thanksgiving dinner.*

1 package fresh cranberries, rinsed and drained

1 navel orange (or other oranges, with seeds removed)

1 cup sugar (or less, to taste)

Put the cranberries and orange (with peeling on, cut into 1-inch square chunks). Place in a food processor and chop until evenly ground. It might be easier to do half at a time.

Put in bowl, stir in sugar to taste. Store covered in refrigerator. (It can also be frozen).

## Easy BBQ Sauce

*This easy barbecue sauce uses ingredients you most likely already have at hand. It can be used on chicken, beef or pork.*

Ketchup
Brown sugar
Vinegar
Mustard
Onion
Garlic
Salt and pepper
Oil

Mix all together in a saucepan, bring to a boil and simmer until thick, stirring often.

Put on roasted meat.

(For pork ribs, for instance, boil the ribs until they are tender. Drain. Put in a roasting pan and add the sauce. Roast at 350 degrees until the ribs look glazed, then turn, add more sauce. Do that a couple of times, until they are glazed to taste.)

# Homemade Eagle Brand milk

1 cup dry nonfat
  powdered milk
1/2 cup warm water
3/4 cup white sugar

Combine dry milk and water. Mix well. Put in top of double boiler over boiling water and add sugar. Stir until sugar is dissolved.

Equal to 1 can of Eagle Brand.

# Homemade Egg Noodles

1, 2 or 3 eggs (depending
  on how many you want
  to make).
1/2 t. salt for each egg
Flour

Whisk together eggs and salt. Add flour, a little at a time, mix to make dough. As soon as it will form into a gob, knead dough until it is no longer sticky. Roll onto a floured board, using extra flour to keep it from sticking to the rolling pin and the rolling surface.

Roll until it is paper thin, sprinkle with flour, roll up and slice into narrow strips. Spread out on board to dry.

To cook: Add a few noodles at a time to boiling water, stew or soup. Boil for 20 minutes.

# Homemade Shake & Bake

*(Makes 4 cups)*

4 cups bread crumbs
1 T. salt
2 t. paprika
1 t. celery salt
1 t. pepper
1/2 t. garlic powder
1/2 t. sage
1 t. onion powder
1/2 cup oil

Mix dry ingredients well and then add oil and mix. Store in air-tight container.

**TO USE:**
Moisten chicken, fish or pork chops and dip in seasoned crumb mixture. Bake in 400-degree oven on greased cookie sheet.

*Over the River …*

# Jerky Marinade

5 pounds beef (fat removed), sliced in 1/4-inch-thick strips
1 cup soy sauce
1 cup water
1 T. Worcestershire sauce
1/2 t. pepper
1/2 t. garlic powder
1/2 t. onion powder
2 T. seasoning salt
4 T. liquid smoke
Tabasco sauce (Optional)

Mix sauce ingredients, pour over meat strips and allow to stand for 8 to 10 hours.

Put on racks in 150-degree oven for 8-10 hours (depending on thickness) until leathery. Put foil or a cookie sheet under the rack to catch the drips.

# Lindbergh Relish

2 medium heads cabbage
8 carrots
12 onions
8 red or green peppers
1/2 cup salt
3 pints vinegar
6 cups sugar
1 t. each celery seed and mustard seed

Grind or chop vegetables and put in a large bowl. Add salt and let stand 2 hours. Drain.

Mix well, put into jars and put on lids and rings, tightened. Keep in a cool place.

*It can be eaten immediately, which is how I like it.*

# Mediterranean Marinade

1/4 cup olive oil
1/4 cup lemon juice
1 t. each salt, marjoram, thyme
1/2 t. pepper
1 clove garlic, minced
1/2 cup chopped onion
1/4 cup snipped parsley

Use to marinate lamb or chicken. This makes enough for about 2 pounds of meat.

For a stronger flavor, substitute balsamic vinegar for the lemon juice. Another option is to switch up the herbs. Try rosemary, oregano, basil.

# Pepper & Green Tomato Relish

8 pounds green tomatoes
6 large onions
3 red or green peppers
1 quart vinegar
2 cups sugar
1 t. turmeric
2 t. celery seed
2 T. whole cloves

Put vegetables through a coarse food grinder. Place in a large bowl and soak in cold water for 3 hours. Drain.

Put in a large kettle and add vinegar and spices. Put the celery seed and cloves in a muslin bag, to be discarded.

Bring to a boil and simmer for 20 minutes.

Pack in jars and seal.

---

# Pickled Crab Apples

4 cups sugar
3/4 cup vinegar
1 cup water
2 T. whole cloves
Cinnamon sticks
1 t. red food coloring

Remove blossom ends from crab apples, but leave the stems. Wash. Wieht a fork, prick apples several times to keep them from bursting. Pack applesinto jars, adding half of a cinnamon stick to each jar.

Boil the other ingredients together for 3 minutes. Add food coloring to the syrup and stir well. Pour syrup over apples in jars. Add lids and rings, tighten. Put in canner and boil for 15 minutes to seal.

**LEFT:** The neighborhood deer family stop by to clean up some of the excess apples in our yard. I'm sure they provided a similar service around several of the crab apple trees nearby and offered to clean up the garden, as well. **ABOVE:** Another visit after the first big snow fall, just in case they missed some.

## TOOLS & TECHNOLOGY

The KitchenAid mixer is my favorite kitchen tool. I got it, I think, in 1979, when I still had the bakery. I used it to make the cookies (See page 117). One batch made about 4 dozen big cookies. We didn't use it for bread then. It's too small for that. The bread was all mixed by hand.

Later, after the bakery closed though, I would use the mixer to make two loaves at a time. And now I have attachments, including a pasta maker, grater and grinder.

My second favorite is probably the small food processor. It holds two or three cups. It's very handy. I use it a lot.

And the hand mixer.

Over the years, new kitchen gadgets were always being given to me. Some were good, others not so much.

Electric can openers have improved. I love the one I have now. Before, they were difficult to clean.

Potato peelers and graters have come a long way. And toasters.

The one thing I've never had, but always wanted was a dishwasher.

But none of those are necessary, really. They're simply time savers.

I have arthritis now, so I have changed the way I do things. But I get them done. Things that I used to just do without thinking I either have to find a work around or ask for help. I hate asking for help.

# Quotable Tips and Hints

■ Cottage cheese and fruit are excellent side dishes that can add color to a meal.

■ Cheese: Take cheese blocks out of plastic and wrap with foil to avoid them molding in the refrigerator.

■ Pineapple: Fresh pineapple tastes so much better than canned, but unless you live in the tropics, finding one that's ready to eat when you buy it is unlikely. Have patience. It can take up to a week. You can tell they're ripe when they start to turn color slightly and smell sweet at the core and the leaves at the top will come loose with a good yank.

■ Bacon: You used to be able to buy jowl bacon, which had a heavier smoky flavor. I haven't seen that in years. Sometimes you can find bacon ends that have a good share of meat to go with the fat. It's great for seasoning vegetables and salads. Everything is better with bacon.

I cook bacon slices in the oven, 325 degrees for 30 minutes.

■ Favorite cookies: molasses, peanut butter and oatmeal. Keep a supply in the freezer for unexpected guests.

■ To dry chicken breasts: Thaw, put pieces on waxed paper, soak up liquid with a paper towel.

■ "Use what you've got." — When I didn't have a rolling pin, I used a large glass bottle. It worked.

■ When using your oven for broiling, make sure you have water in the bottom of the broiling pan, which cuts the grease splatter and makes clean up easier.

■ Extra green or red peppers can be chopped and put into quart-size freezer bags for use later.

■ Freezer bags: For those with arthritis, the zipper bags work well.

■ When I cooked at the YMCA summer camp, we had access to "commodities" distributed by the U.S. Department of Agriculture, things like cornmeal and peanut butter, which allowed the organization to cut its food budget if we could come up with recipes using the ingredients that the children would eat. We were serving about 100 campers breakfast, lunch and dinner.

The favorites included cornmeal cake with peanut butter frosting and peanut butter pie.

■ "I always do one more," whether that's an extra slice of bacon being chopped for green beans or …

■ All stoves are different, so keep a close eye.

■ "I'm a firm believer in making two of everything. Freeze one for later."

■ When starting to bake, fill the sink with water and drop in your tools when you are done with them to make clean up easier.

■ "Sometimes you have to use your imagination." … The comment after putting the rhubarb cake in the oven, sitting down on the porch and falling asleep. "The cake was a little crunchy, but still edible. But I made some Nantucket Pudding as a back up, just in case."

■ "Rinse, rinse, rinse. That's the way to go."

*See page 142 for "More hints I learned the hard way."*

*Over the River …*

# Gift Ideas

*Homemade treats make wonderful gifts for birthdays and during the holidays, as well as for thank yous for neighbors and friends during the year. You can buy fun fancy tins, but empty coffee cans, decorated for the occasion, work well to keep the goodies from getting crushed.*

## Albert's Caramel Corn

2 cups brown sugar
1/2 pound butter (2 cubes)
1/2 cup white corn syrup (Karo Syrup)
1 t. salt
6 quarts popped corn
1 t. soda

Boil together first four ingredients for 5 minutes. Stir in soda and quickly add to popped corn (use a greased spoon and a large bowl). Keep stirring until corn is coated.

Dump into a large baking pan (with sides) and bake one hour in 200-degree oven, stirring every 5 minutes.

Cool on waxed paper. Store in air-tight container.

## Betty's Dipped Coconut Chocolates

1 cube butter, melted
1 pound powdered sugar
1 small package coconut
1 can sweetened condensed milk
1/2 cup finely chopped walnuts
1 12-ounce package chocolate chips
1/2 block paraffin wax

Mix all together and form into small balls. Place on a cookie sheet and put in the freezer until hard.

Melt chocolate chips in a pan or bowl over hotwater. Add paraffin. Stir. When melted and mixed together, dip each ball in the chocolate and place on waxed paper to cool.

---

## Good and Easy Caramels

1 cup butter or margarine
1 pound brown sugar
Pinch of salt
1 cup white corn syrup
1 15-ounce can sweetened condensed milk
1 t. vanilla
**Optional add-ins**
1 cup coconut, chopped citron and/or nuts

Melt butter in a heavy 3-quart sauce pan. Add brown sugar and salt. Stir until thoroughlycombined. Stir in corn syrup, mix well. Gradually add milk, stirring constantly. Cook and stir over medium heat until thermometer reaches 245 degrees. Remove from heat, stir in vanilla. Mix in coconut, citron or nuts if desired. Pour into a 9x9" buttered pan. Cool, cut into squares.

## Hand-Dipped Ritzies

1 package Almond Bark (any flavor)
Ritz crackers
Peanut butter

### More gift ideas:

   Melt almond bark in double boiler. Spread peanut butter on crackers and squeeze together to make sandwiches. Try to make sure peanut butter is even with the edge of the crackers, but doesn't ooze out.

   Using two forks or tongs, dip cracker sandwiches into melted bark, making sure they are covered. Place on waxed paper and top with sprinkles or nuts. Let them sit for several hours until set. Trim off excess coating.

# More Hints I Learned the Hard Way

*(This is a continuation of the list of hints I started in The Red Cabin Cookbook)*

■ I found it hard to cook for three people when I cooked for more for so long. Freezing is a good way to solve the abundance of leftovers problem.

■ Soups and stews can be made, cooled and frozen in containers or double plastic bags, in the right amount for as many as you feed on regular basis.

■ Cooked potatoes can be frozen for convenience, then thawed and heated in foil in the oven.

■ Freeze cooked spaghetti noodles in plastic bags. When ready to use, remove noodles from bag and put in a pot of boiling water and cover. Turn off the heat and let it sit until thawed. Turn on the heat and bring to a boil. Drain and serve with sauce.

■ If you have canned prunes or plums that are not being used up, try a cobbler made with the pitted prunes, adding the juice and grated orange rind. I also put in some red food coloring.

■ Sprinkle granulated sugar on top of your meringue before putting it in the oven and your knife won't stick when you cut it.

■ Grease your pie pans before putting your dough in and your pie is not as likely to get soggy on the bottom.

■ A small natural-bristle paint brush is perfect for greasing the tops of bread and rolls. It's also great for basting.

■ Grate cheese onto a plate that has been rinsed with cold water and the cheese will slide right off.

■ Sift flour and other dry baking ingredients into a paper plate, bend the plate for easy pouring and no mess.

■ Add a few drops of lemon juice to the water in which you cook rice. The rice will be really white and the lemon juice keeps the grains whole.

■ To easily cut dates and marshmallows, dip your scissors in hot water.

■ When serving gingerbread, try a couple of tablespoons of molasses instead of vanilla in your whipped cream.

■ Tape recipes you use regularly to the inside of your cupboard door.

■ When breading meat, chicken or fish, dip it first in flour, then egg and then crumbs.

■ To reheat biscuits or rolls, put them in a wet paper bag. Fasten tightly and put in a pre-heated 350-degree oven for 10 mInutes.

■ For a fast shine on boots or shoes, cut a lemon and rub it over the leather. Wipe off quickly with a soft cloth.

■ Remove odors from bottles or jars by filling them with a solution of water and dry mustard. Let stand for several hours and rinse in hot water.

■ To remove the tarnish from copperware, clean it with half a lemon dipped in a mixture of 1 tablespoon each salt and vinegar.

■ Clean varnished floors and woodwork with cold tea to bring out the shine.

■ For easier cleaning, douse fresh fish in hot salted water until the scales curl.

■ Wipe your cheese grater with salad oil before grating cheese. It keeps the cheese from sticking and makes the grater easier to clean.

# How much?

15 crushed graham crackers makes 1 cup of crumbs.
A 2-pound chicken makes 2 1/2 cups of cooked, diced chicken.
5 whole eggs = 1 cup.
8-9 egg whites = 1 cup.
12 egg yolks = 1 cup.
1 pound raw unpeeled potatoes = 2 cups cooked, mashed potatoes.
1 cup raw rice + 3 cups cooked.
1 medium onion = 1/2 cup, chopped.
1 small can evaporated milk = 2/3 cup
1 large can evaporated milk = 1 2/3 cups.
1 can sweetened condensed milk (Eagle Brand) = 1 1/3 cups.
1/2 pound of spaghetti, macaroni or noodles = 4 cups cooked.
1 envelope unflavored gelatin = 1 tablespoon.
1/4 pound cheddar cheese = 1 cup grated.
1 pound apples = 3 medium apples.
1 medium apple = 1 cup sliced.
3-4 slices of dry bread = 1 cup fine bread crumbs.
1 pound tomatoes = 3 medium tomatoes.
1 16-ounce package of raisins = 3 cups.
1 pound shortening = 2 1/2 cups.
1 medium lemon = 2-3 tablespoons juice.
1 pound flour = 4 cups sifted.
1 pound butter or margarine = 2 cups
5 pounds granulated sugar = 15 cups.
1 pound powdered sugar = 4 cups.
1 pound brown sugar = 2 1/2 cups.
5 pounds all-purpose flour = 20 cups.
5 pounds whole wheat flour = 18 1/3 cups.
1/4-ounce dry yeast = 1 tablespoon.
8 cups corn flakes = 3 cups crushed crumbs.

### Food for a crowd

**Sandwiches:** 1 loaf sandwich bread makes 20 sandwiches.
**Cakes:** 1 medium-size cake can be cut into 20 pieces.
**Butter:** 1 pound will make 50 sandwiches.
**Coffee:** 1/2 pound makes 20 cups.
**Ice cream:** 1 gallon serves 20 people; 1 quart brick serves 8.
**Meats:** 35 pounds of any meat will serve 100 people.
**Chicken:** A 3-pound chicken serves 6 if fried; 8 if creamed.
**Salad:** 1 gallon serves 34 people.
**Vegetables:** 1 gallon serves 36 to 40.
**Hamburger or meat loaf:** 10 pounds serves 50 people.

# Substitutions

| | | |
|---|---|---|
| 1 tablespoon corn starch | = | 2 tablespoons flour |
| 1 teaspoon baking powder | = | 1/3 teaspoon baking soda, 1/2 teaspoon cream of tartar, 1/8 teaspoon salt |
| 1-ounce square of baking chocolate | = | 3 tablespoons cocoa plus 1-1/2 tablespoons shortening |
| 1 cup cake flour | = | 1 cup, less 2 tablespoons, all-purpose flour |
| 1 cup buttermilk or sour milk | = | 1 cup sweet milk plus 1 tablespoon vinegar or lemon juice |

**Bread:** 5 loaves serves 50 people.
**Rolls:** 6 to 8 dozen serves 50 people.
**Potatoes:** 12 pounds of potatoes, mashed, serves 50 people.

### Weights and Measures

3 teaspoons = 1 tablespoon
16 tablespoons = 1 cup
2 tablespoons - 1 ounce (liquid)
2 cups = 1 pint
16 ounces = 1 pound
1 cup = 1/2 pint

### 1 pound equals …

4 cups flour
2 cups butter
2 cups granulated sugar
3 1/3 cups powdered sugar
2 1/2 cups brown sugar
3 cups corn meal
4 cups grated cheese
2 cups uncooked rice
2 cups raisins
4 cups shelled walnuts
2 cups dry beans
2 cups bread crumbs
2 cups chopped meat
4 cups macaroni
4 cups cocoa
2 cups lard
4 cups oatmeal
16 squares baking chocolate

# Index

The barn, back field and old bus (that Neval and his brothers used as their home-away-from-home when they were logging) are part of the tour visitors and family members take when they come to visit. These photos are from a pre-Thanksgiving walk in 2015, that got people out of the house for a while so the cooks could finish dinner preparations.

*Over the River ...*

# What now?

The problem with cookbooks,
of course, is that as soon
as they're finished, you come up
with new recipes.
For those who want to keep up
with the latest, go to

## www.grandmasplaincooking.com

Some of the kids, grandkids and a couple great grandchildren help celebrate my 89th birthday on July 26, 2018. Potato salad was on the menu. Some things never change. Pictured, back row from left, Kimberly McDaniels, Shadee Berger, Daysha Eaton, Bill Granzer, Luke Eaton (standing tall), Stephan McDaniels, Nevonne McDaniels, Kelly McDaniels and Adam Granzer. On the bench, from left, Tilly Hamachek, Julius Eaton, Pat Harris and Muriel Eaton.

*Over the River …*

Made in the USA
Las Vegas, NV
14 October 2021